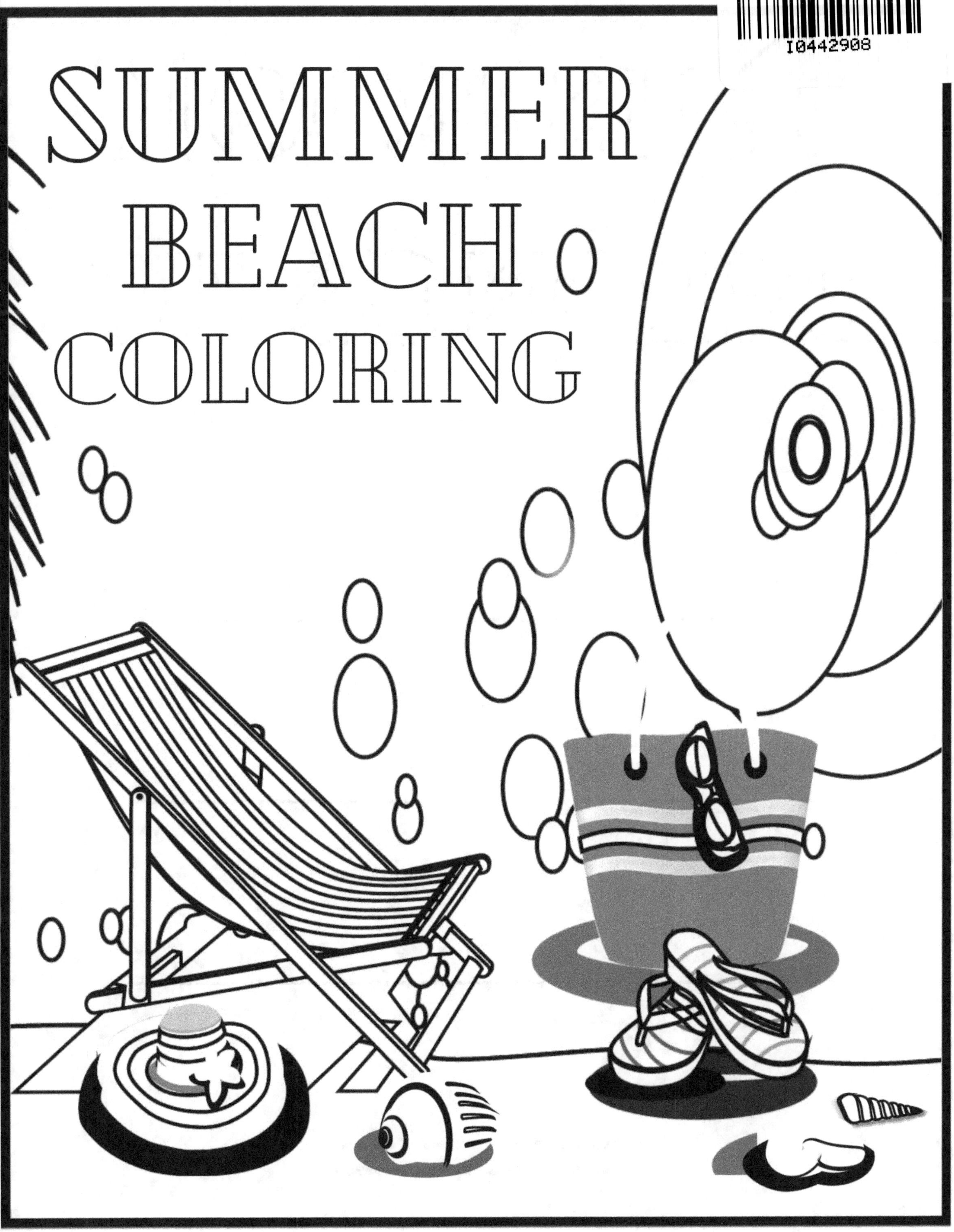
SUMMER
BEACH
COLORING

THIS BOOK BELONGS TO

____

____

____

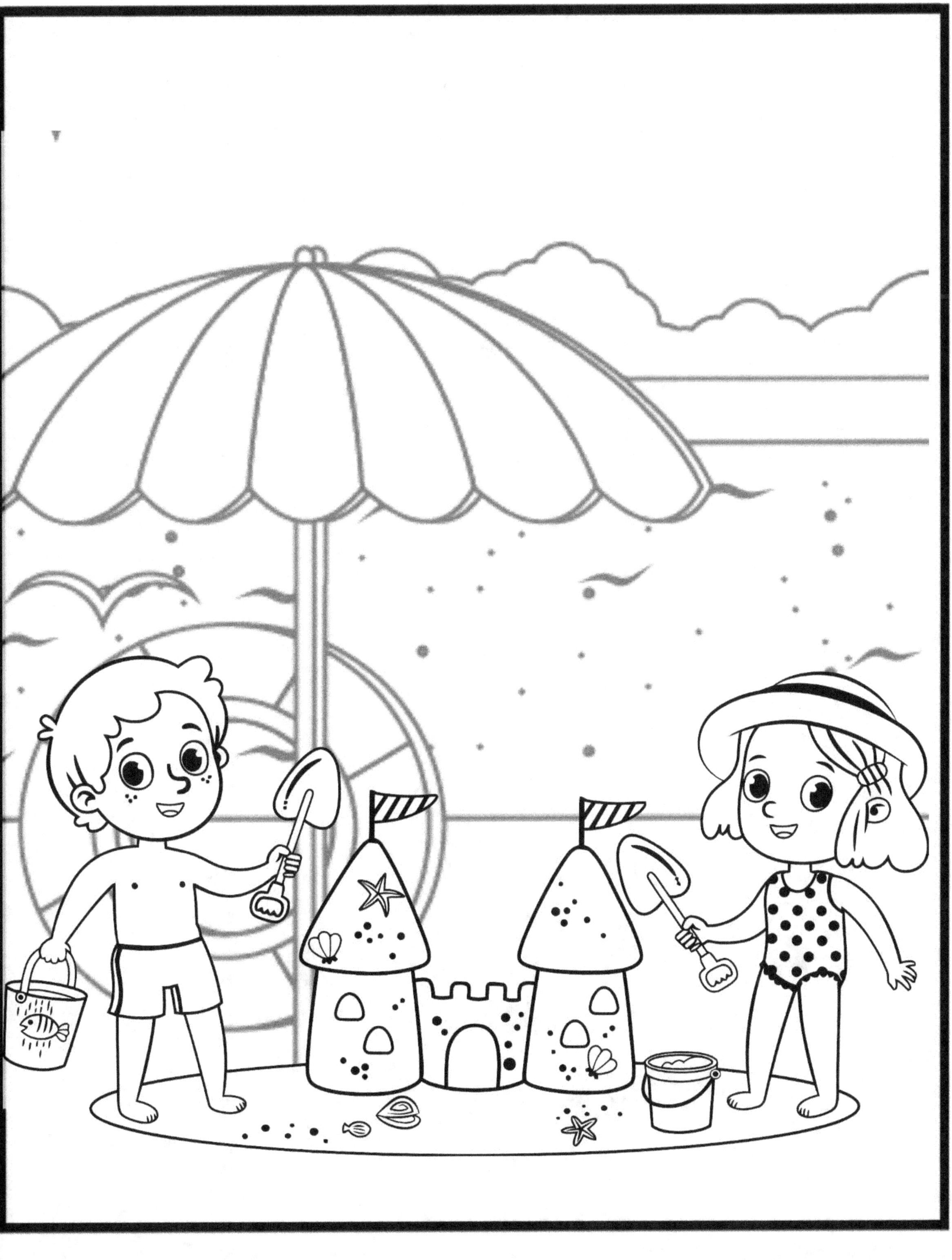

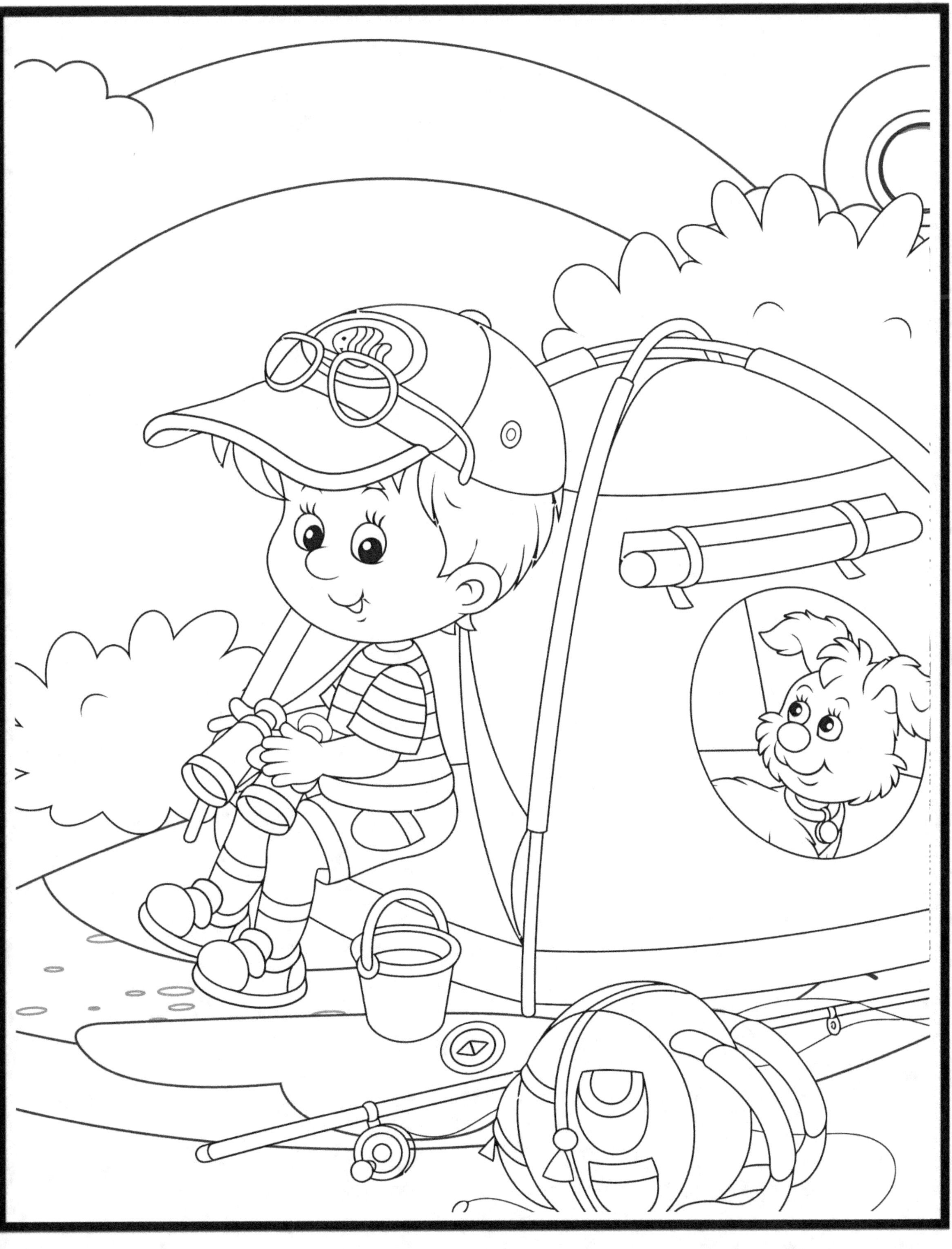

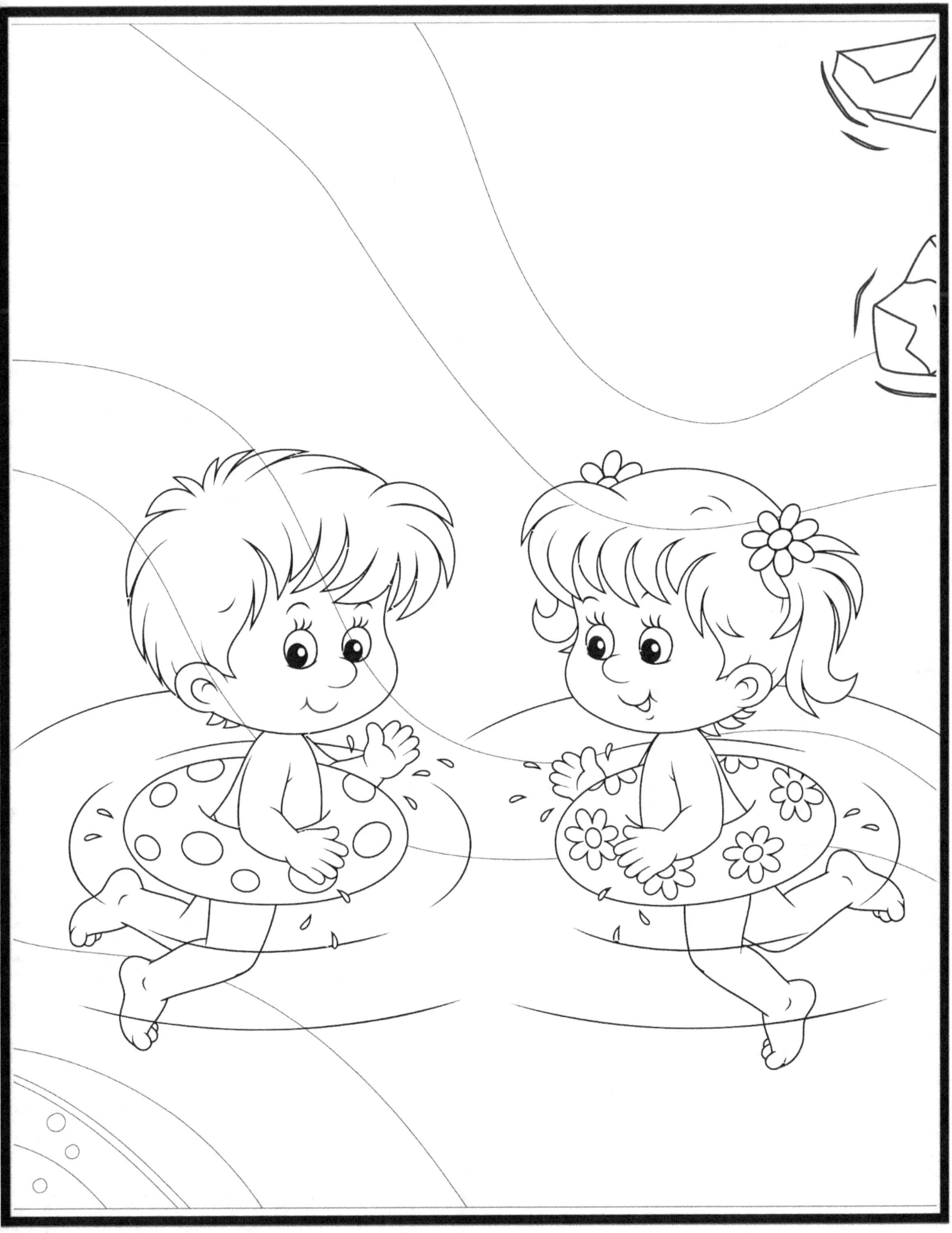

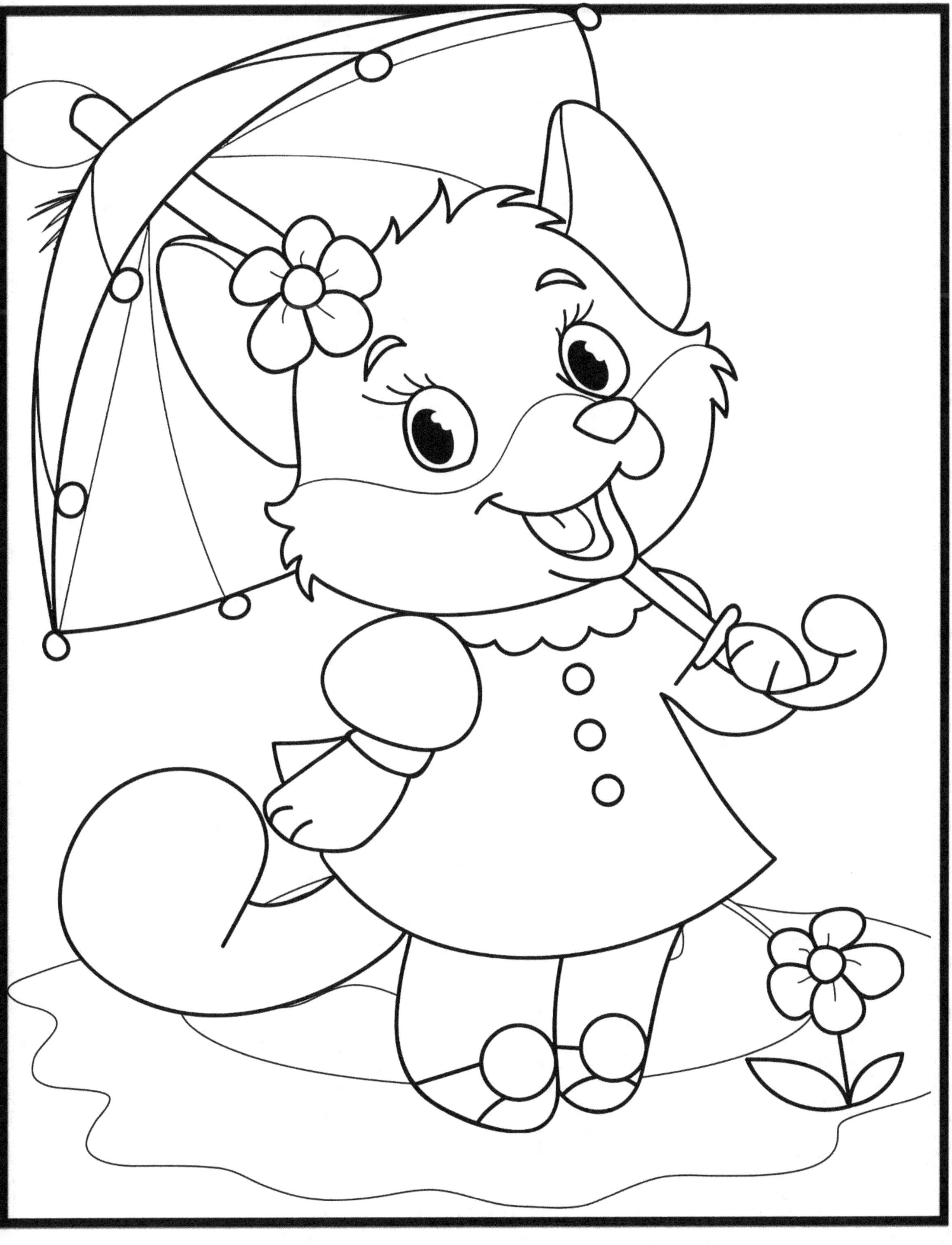

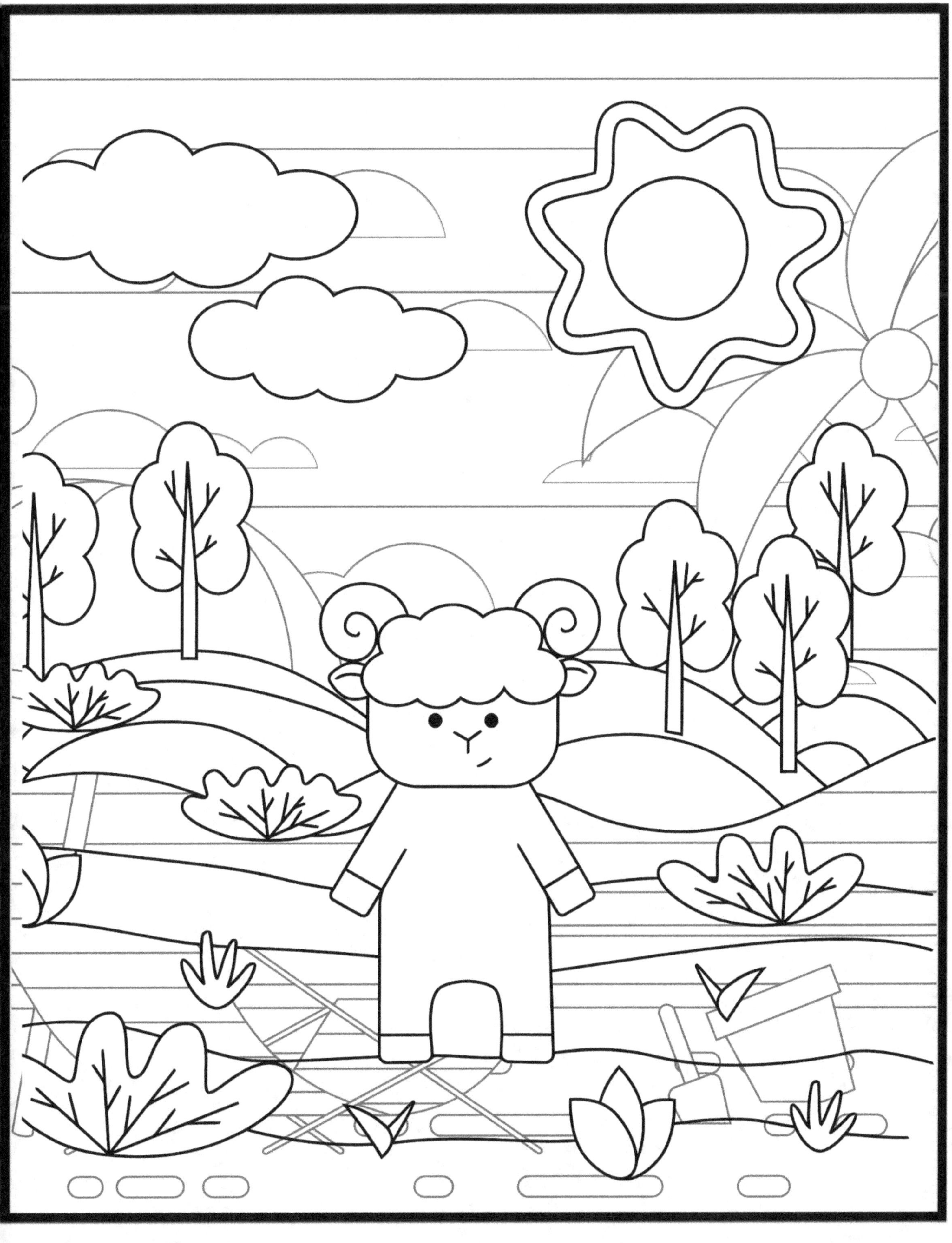

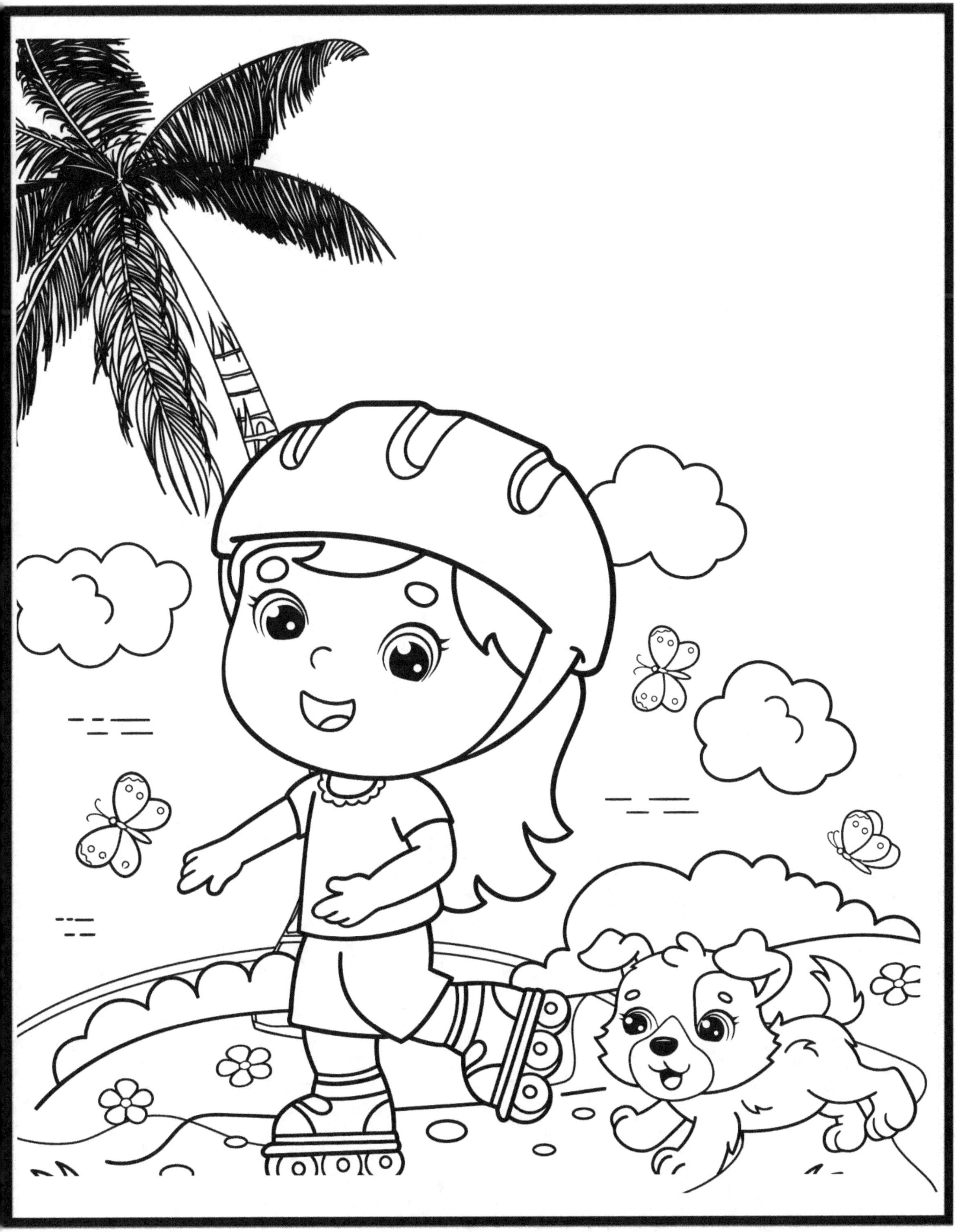

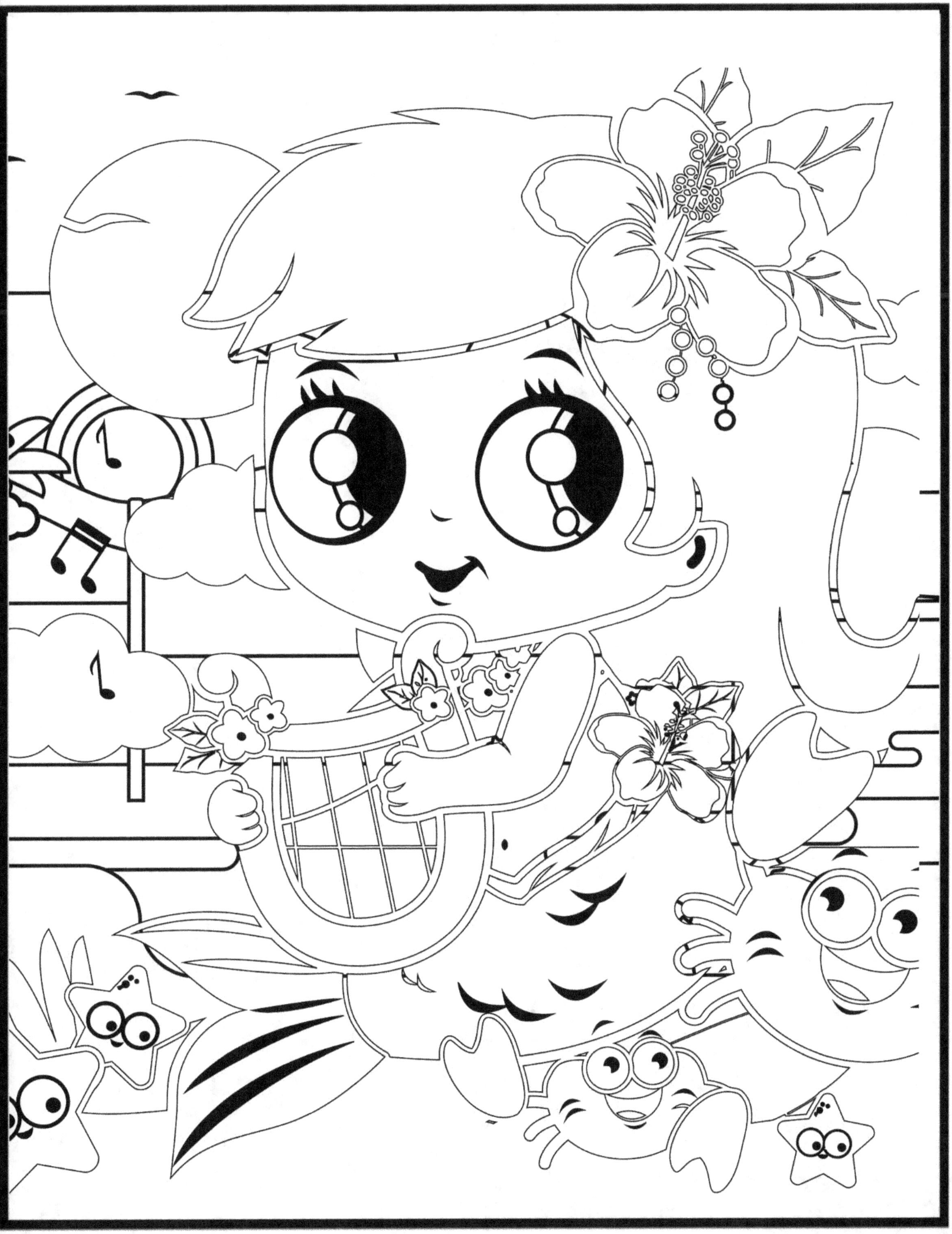

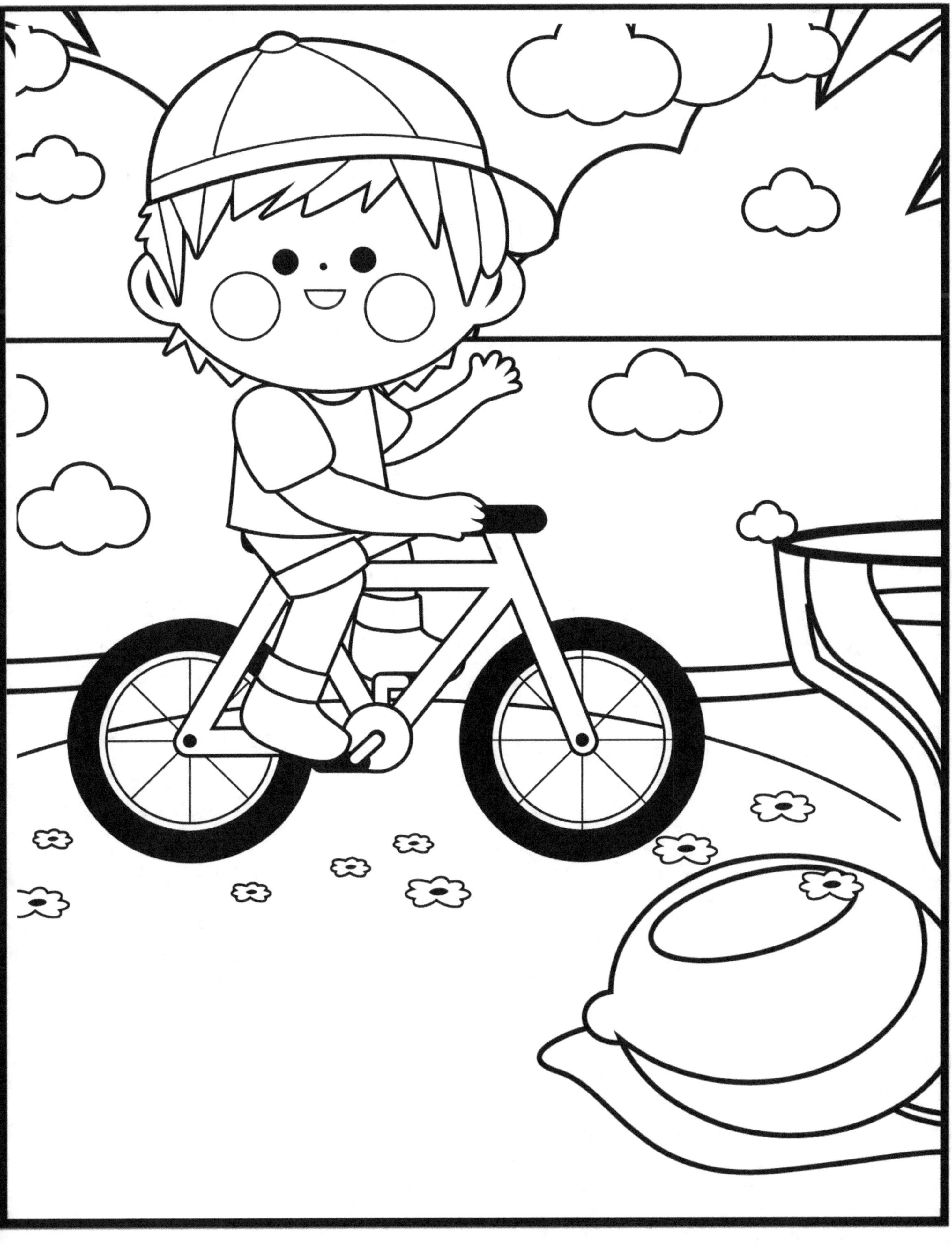

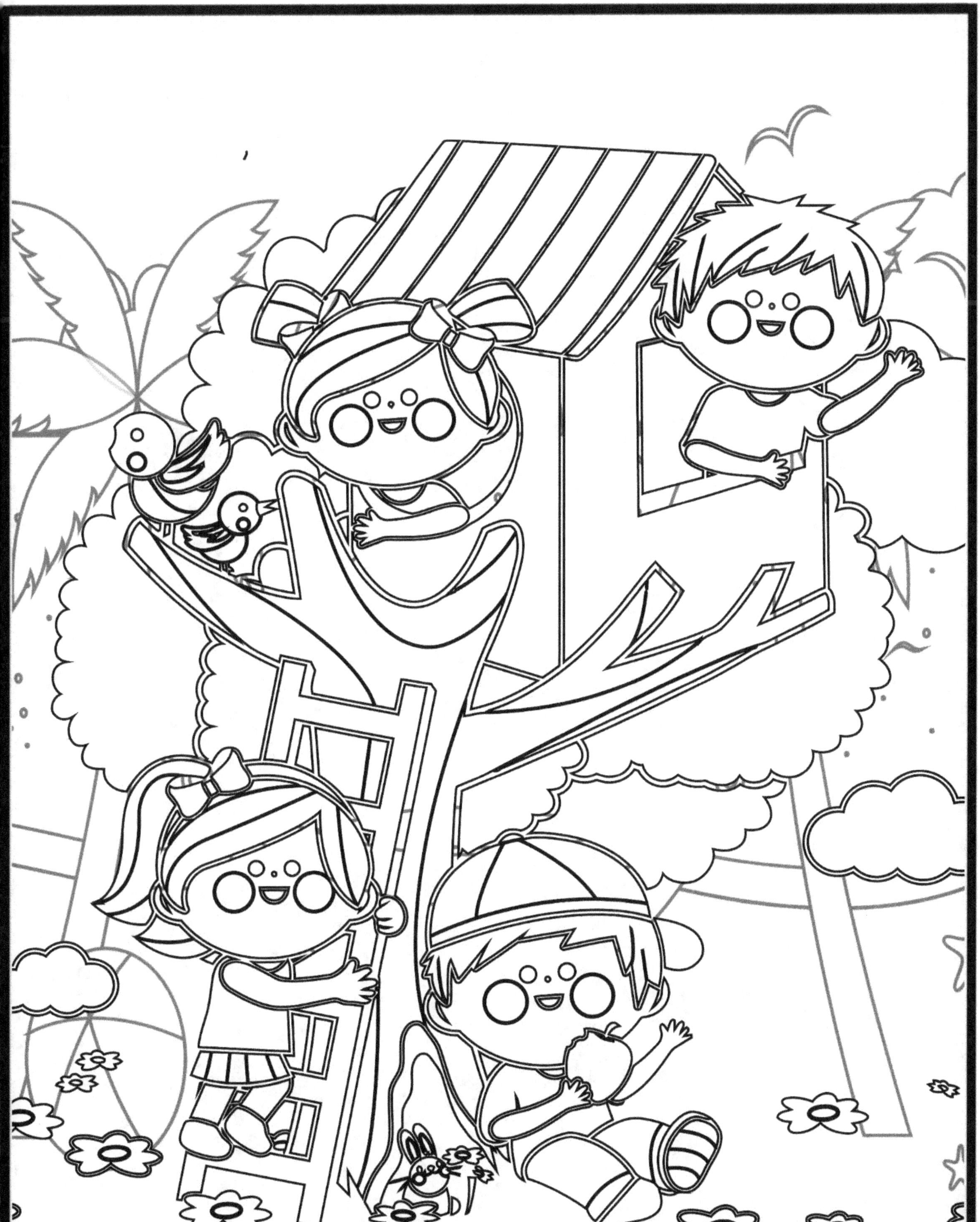

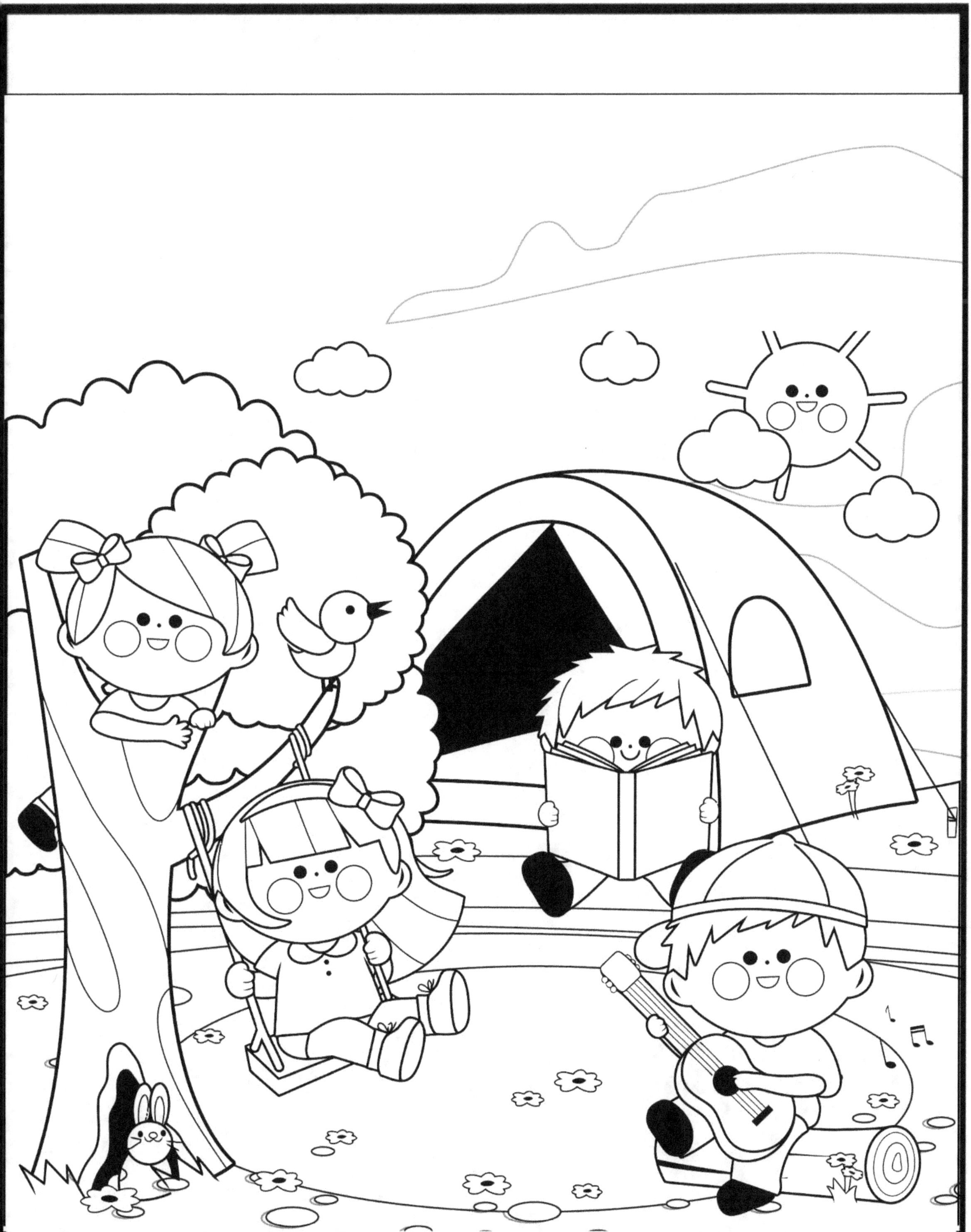

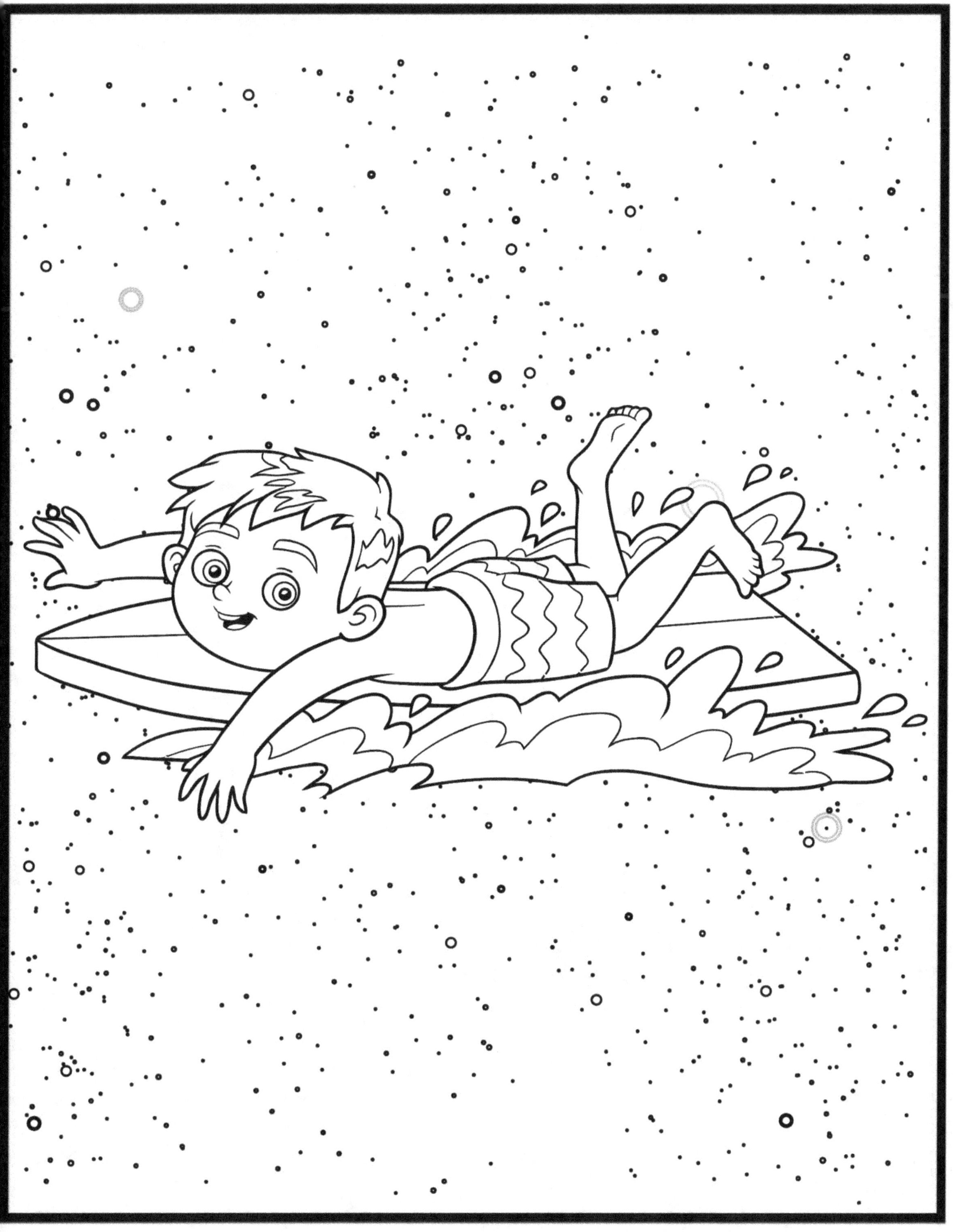

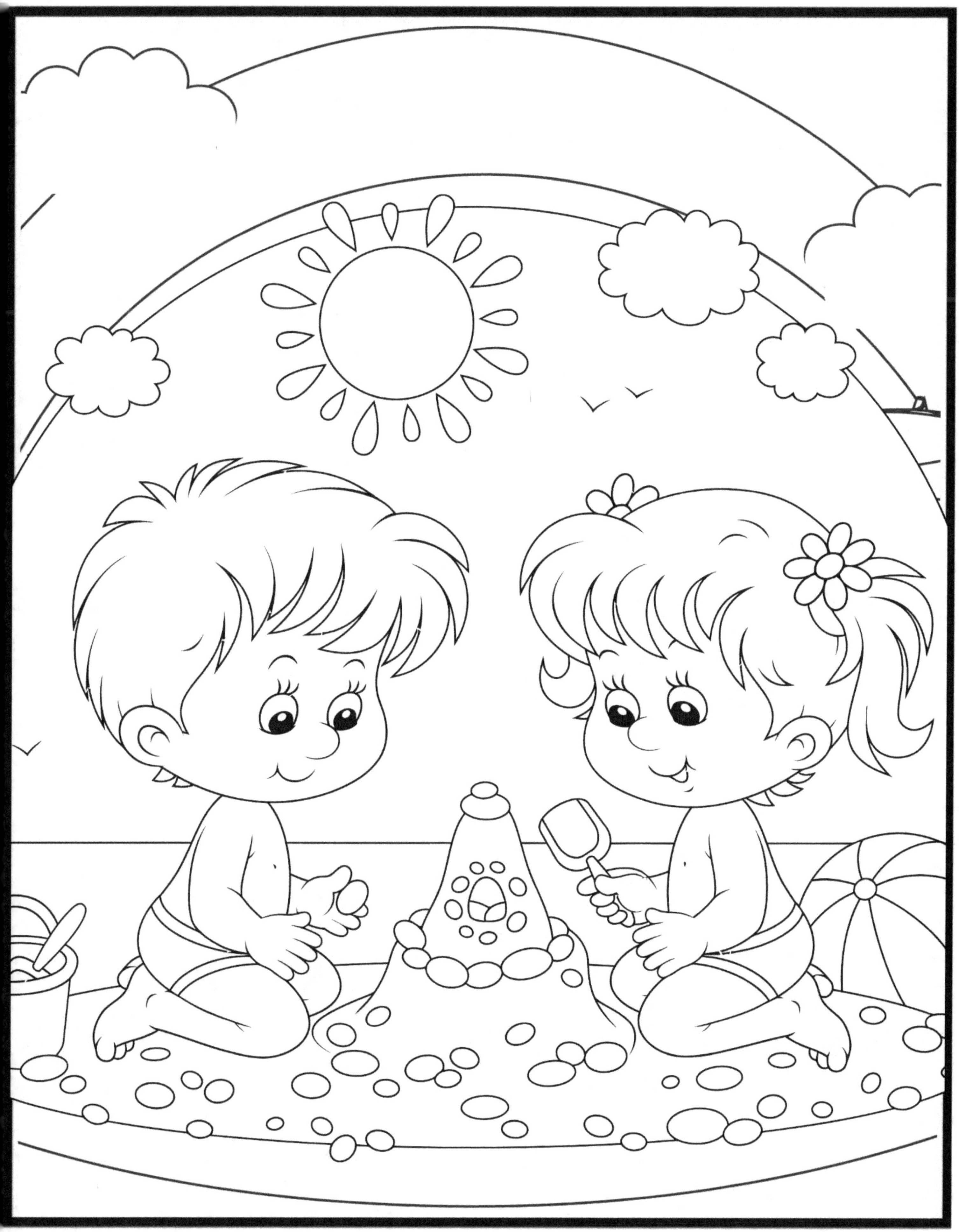

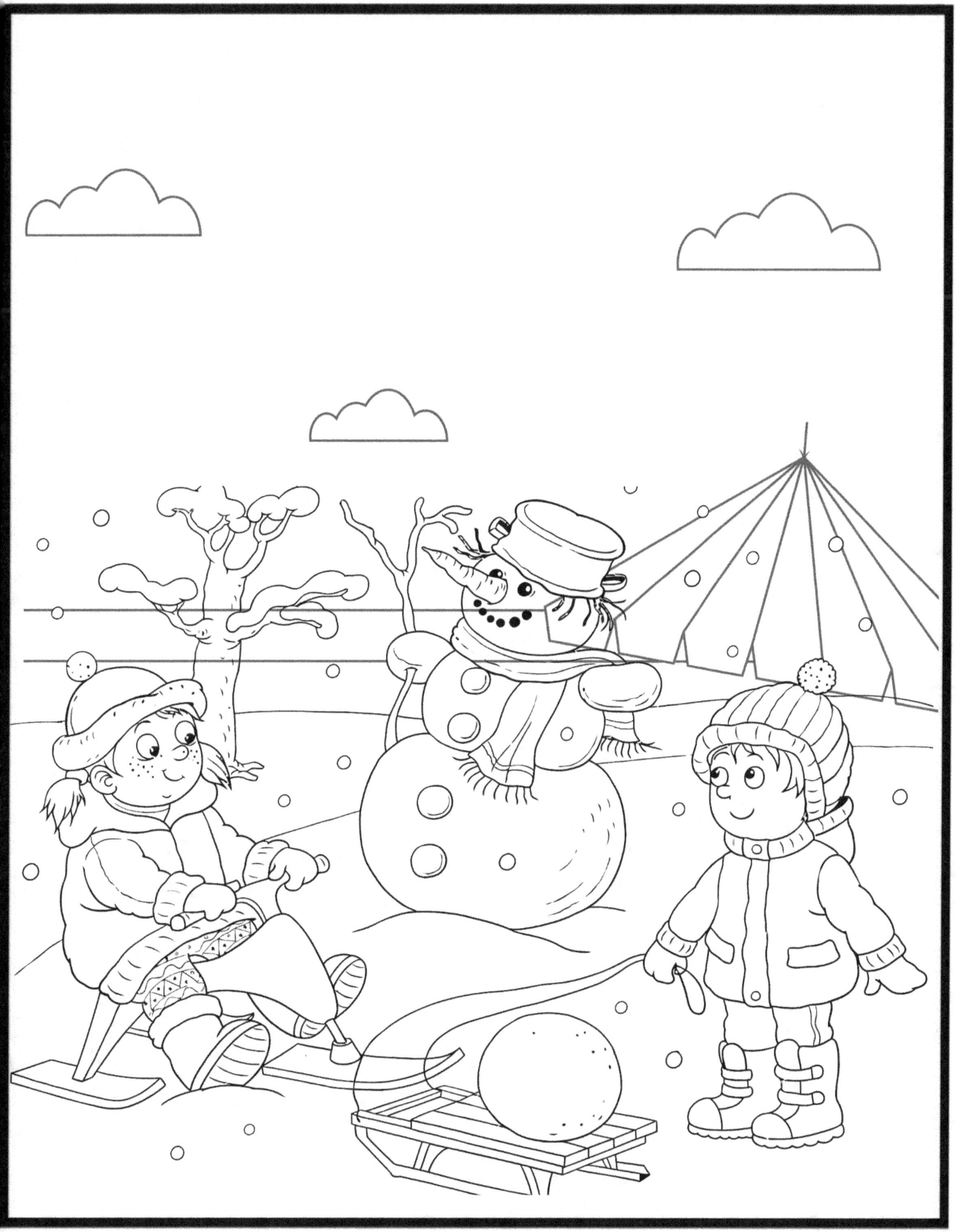

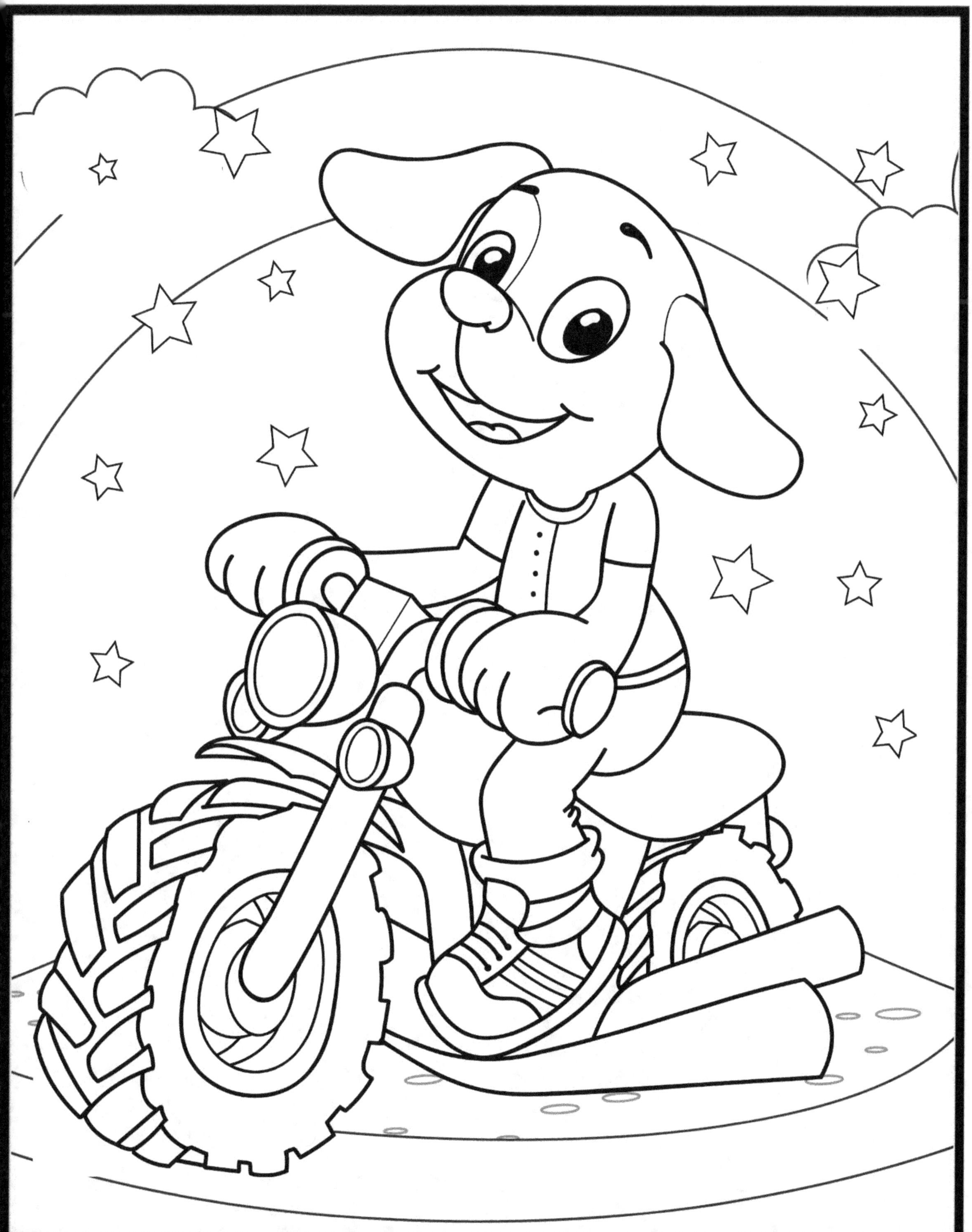

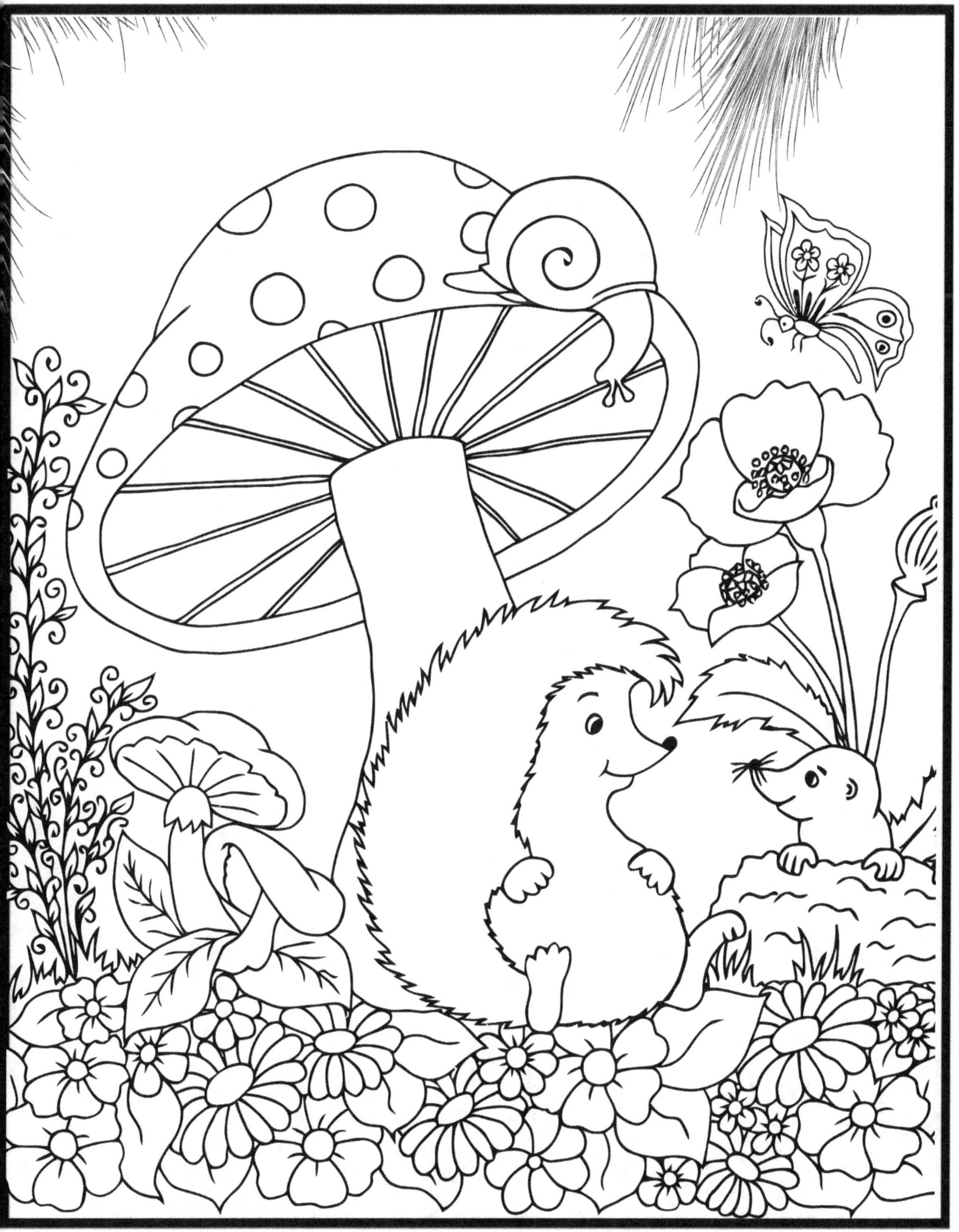

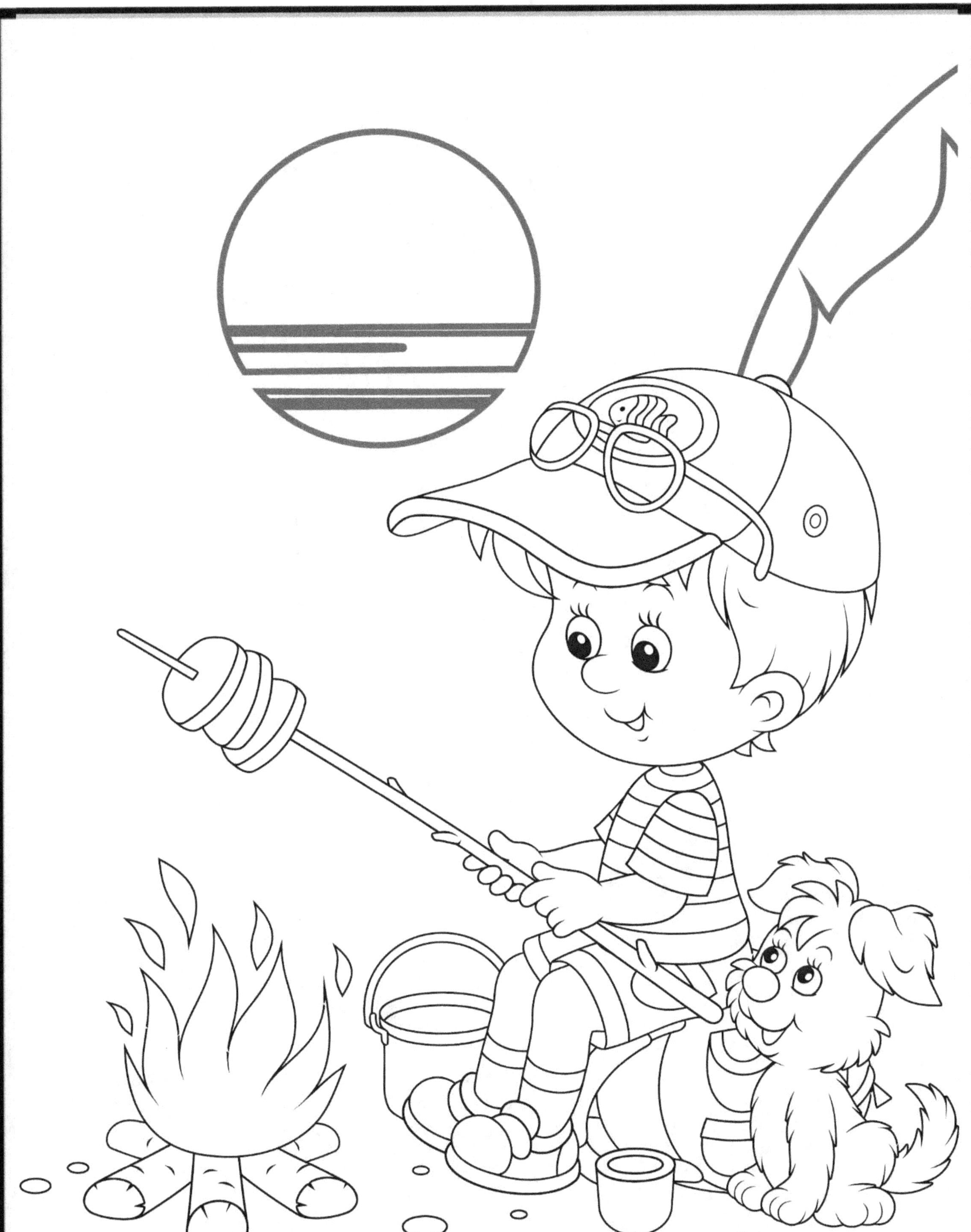

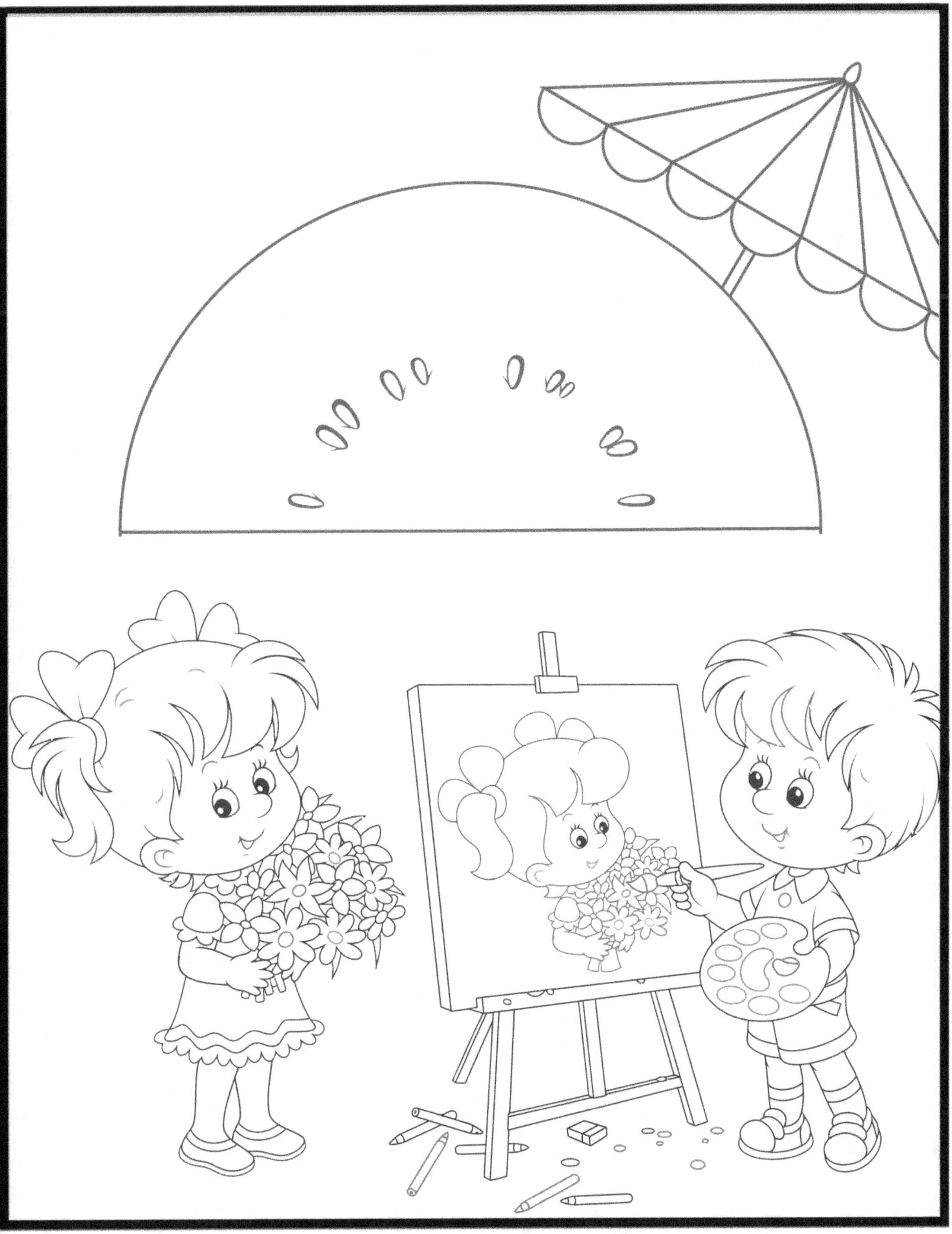

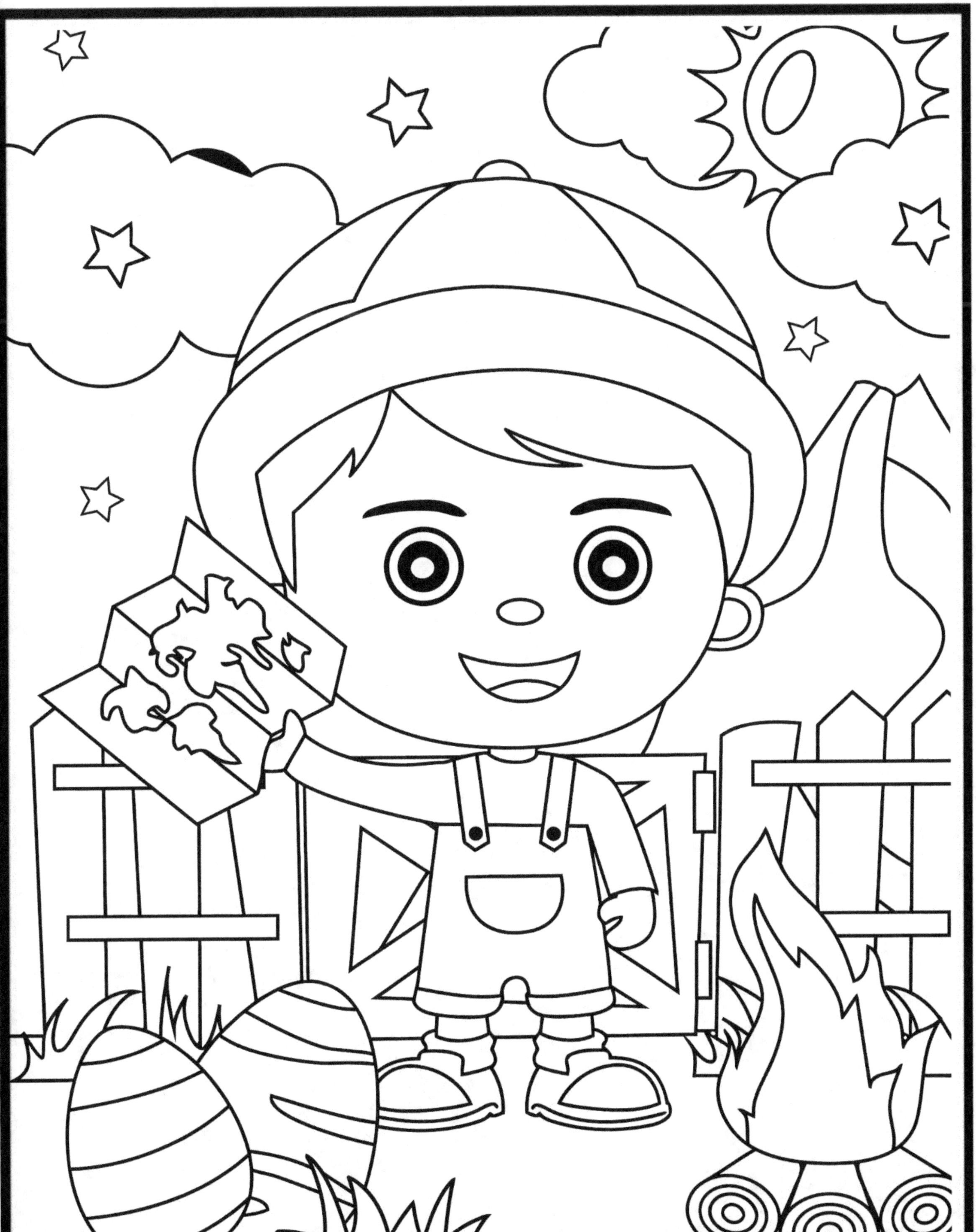

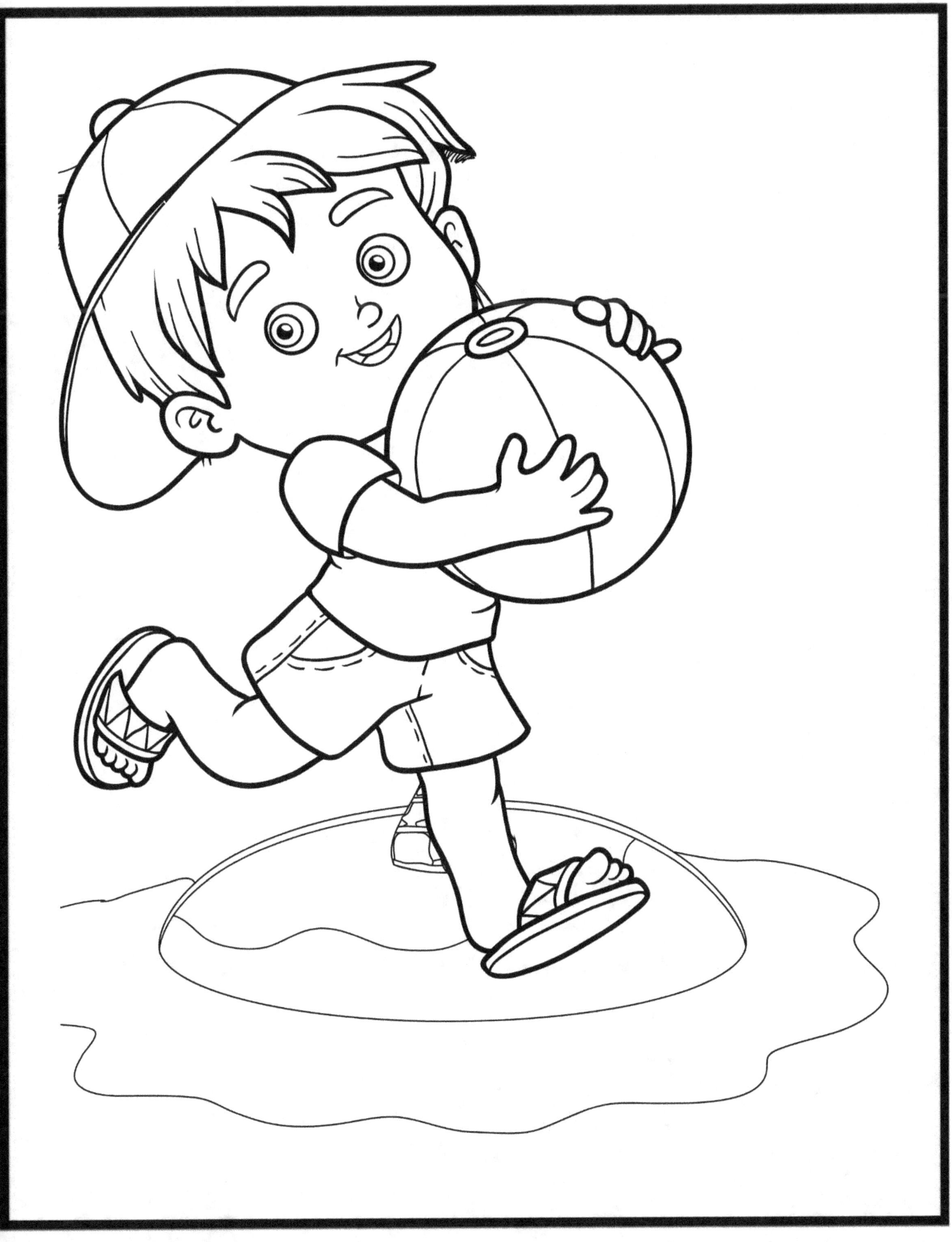

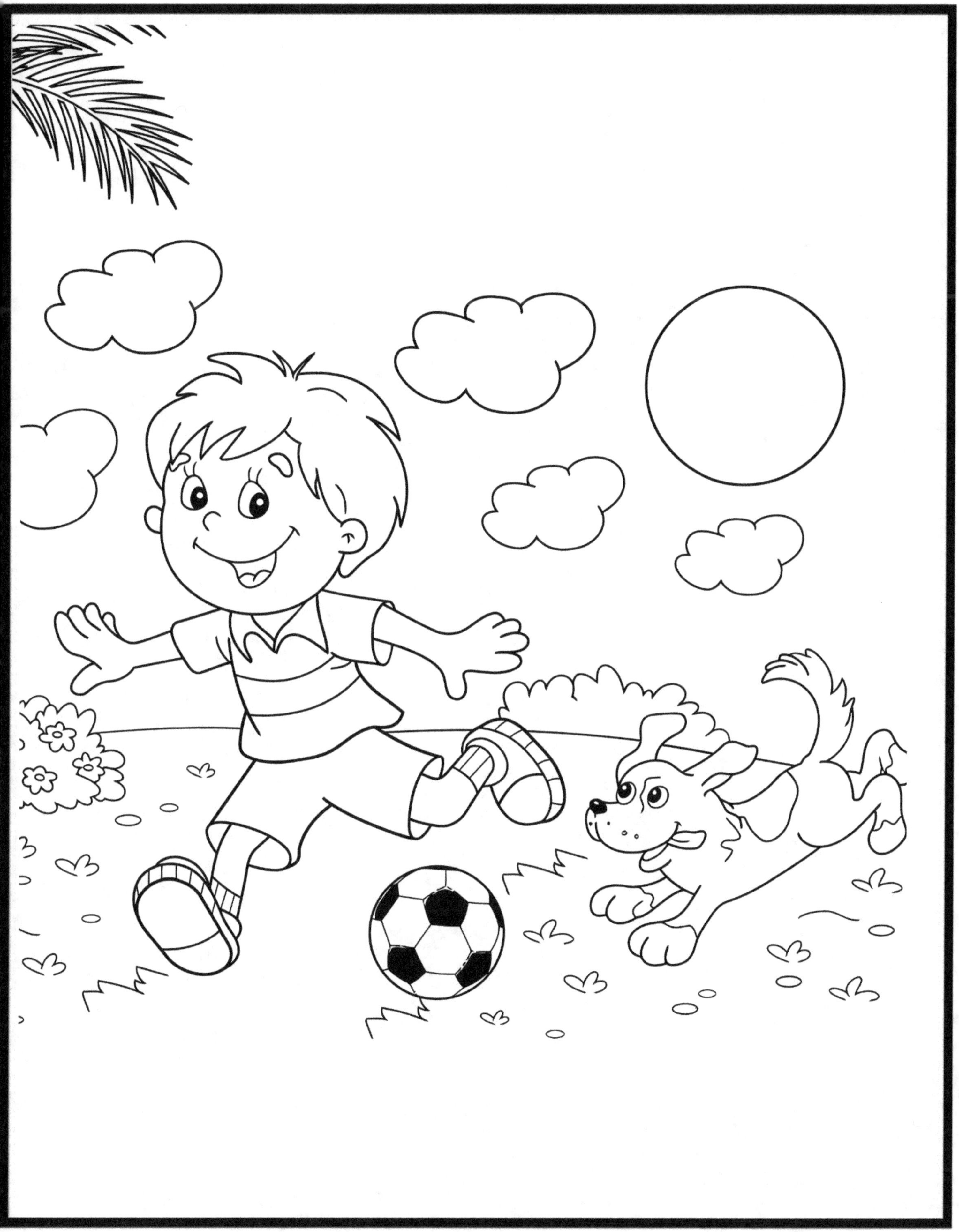

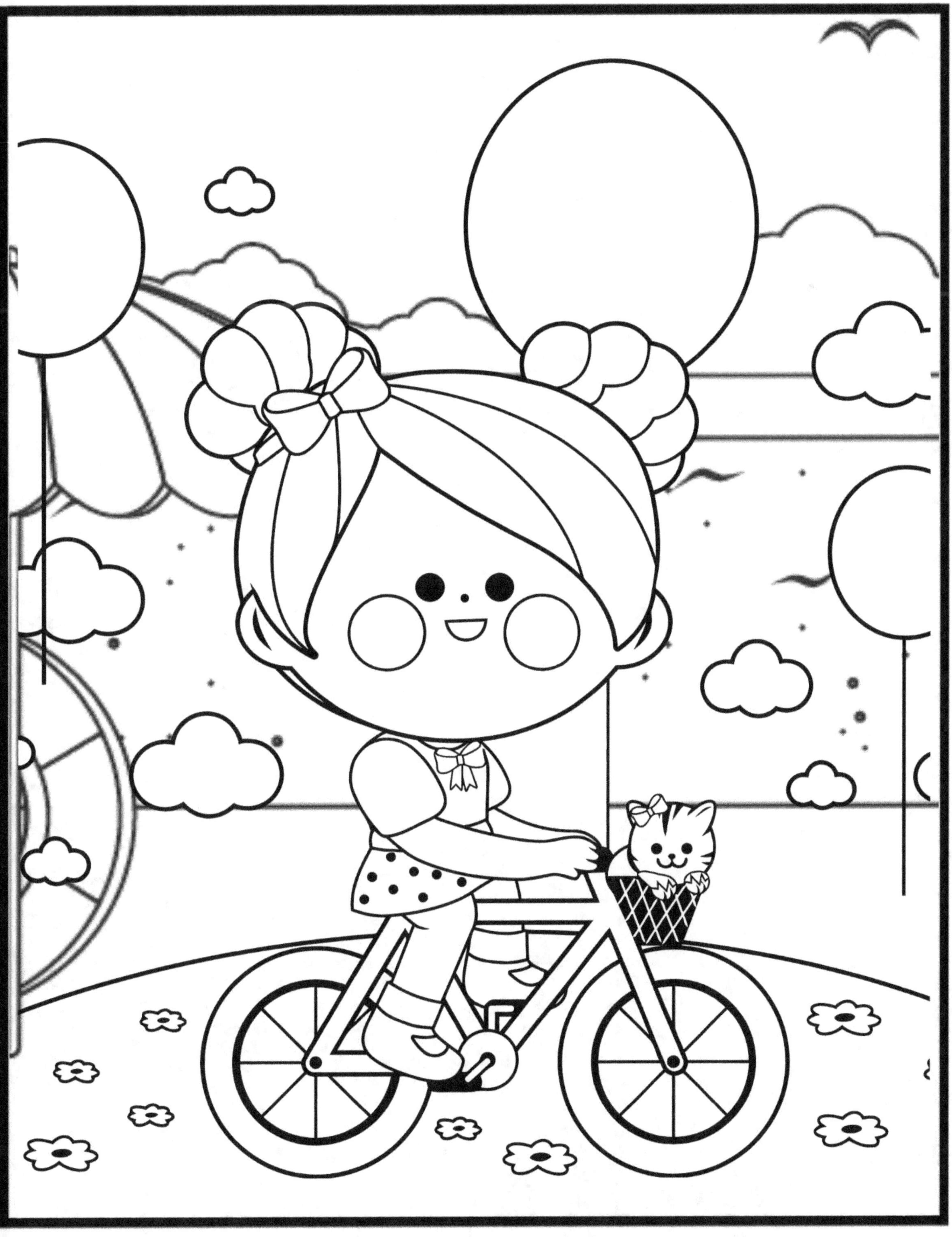

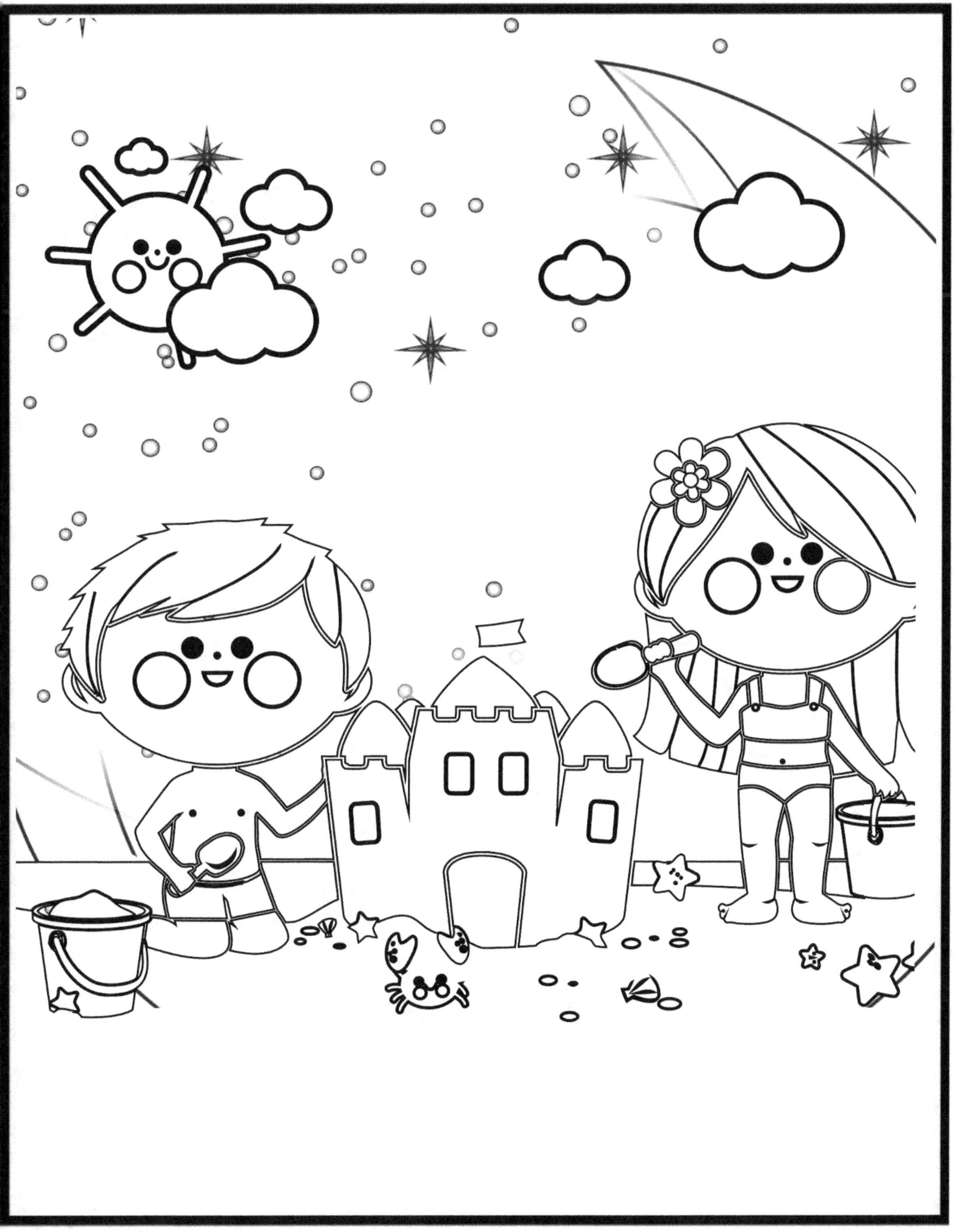

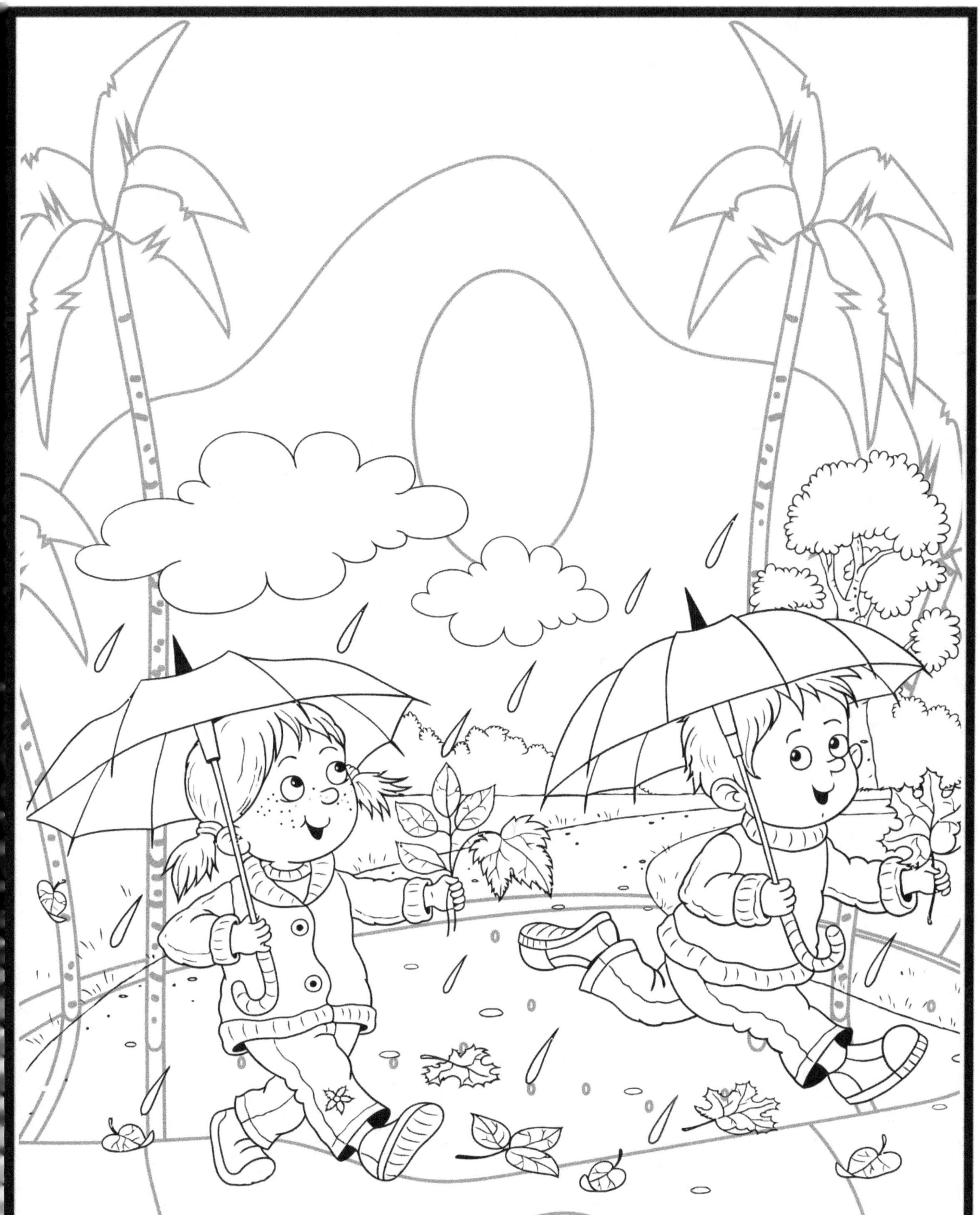

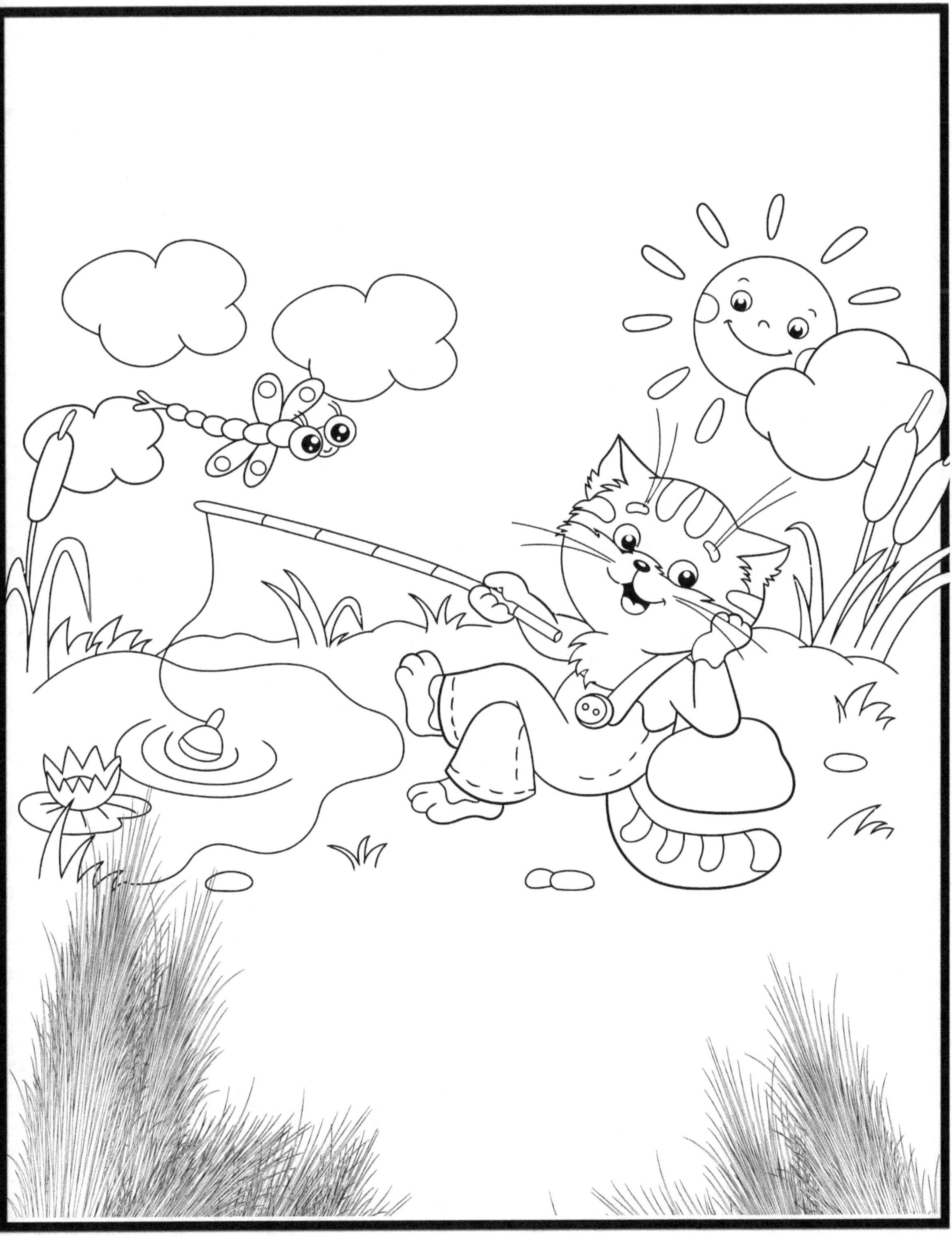

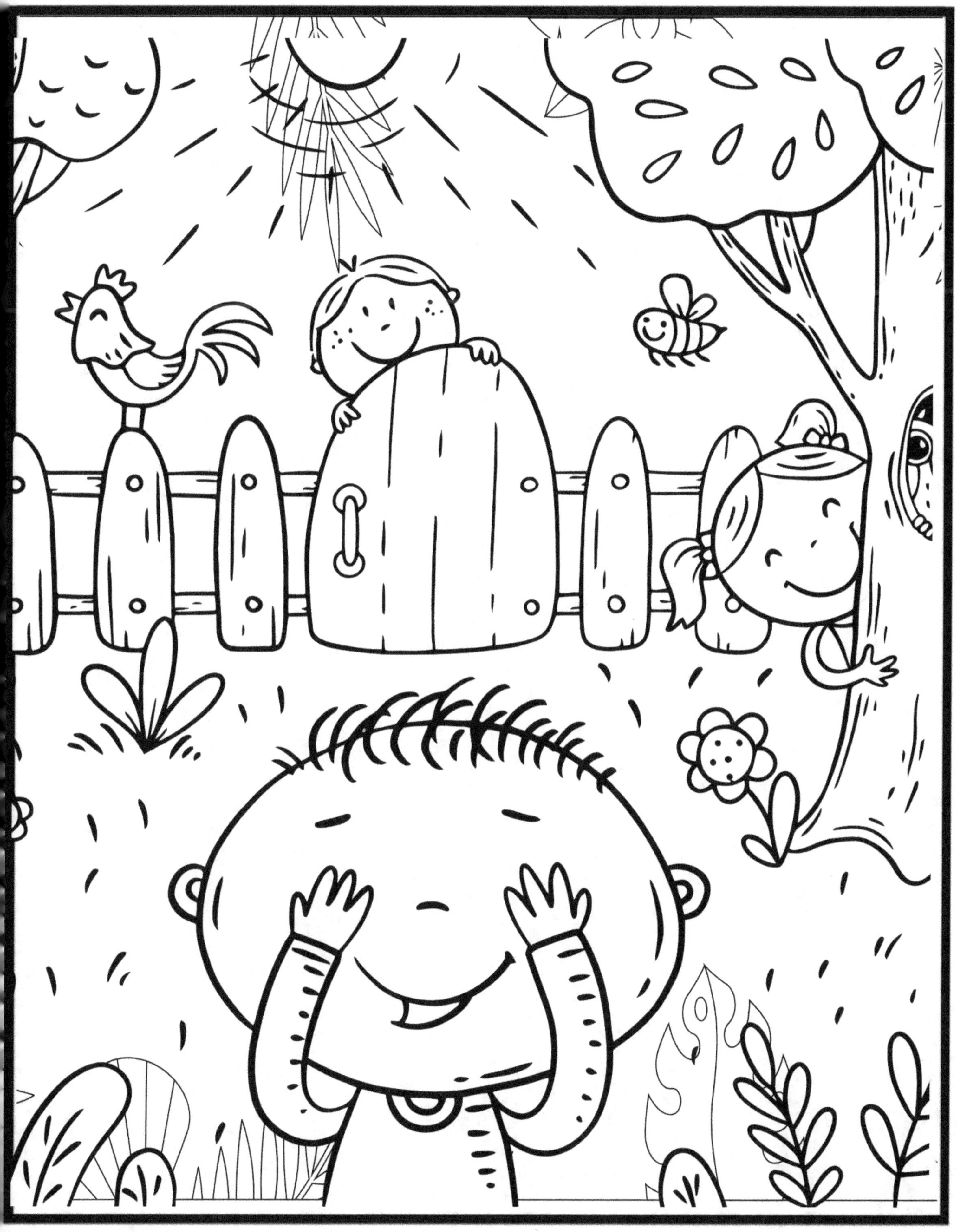

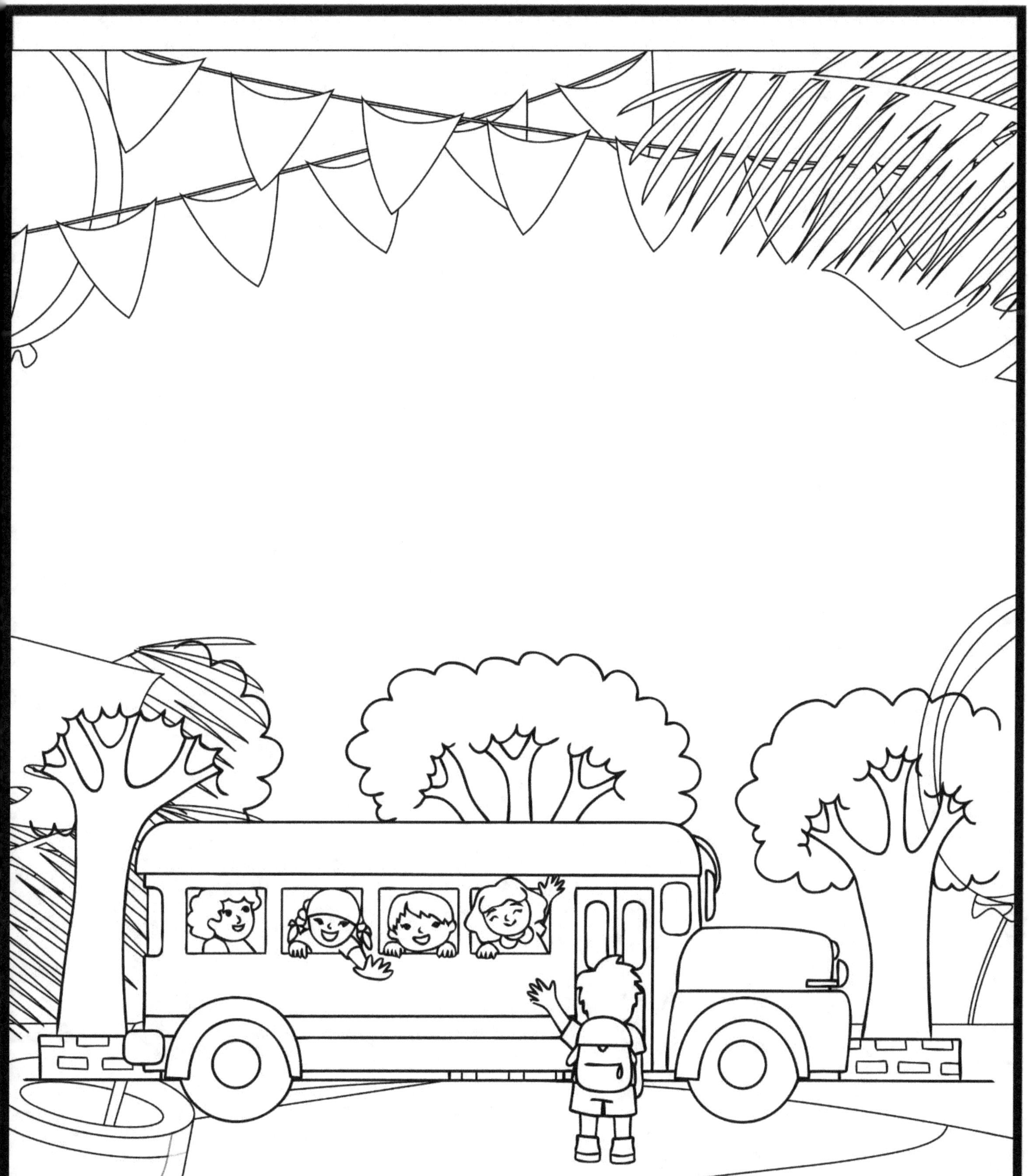

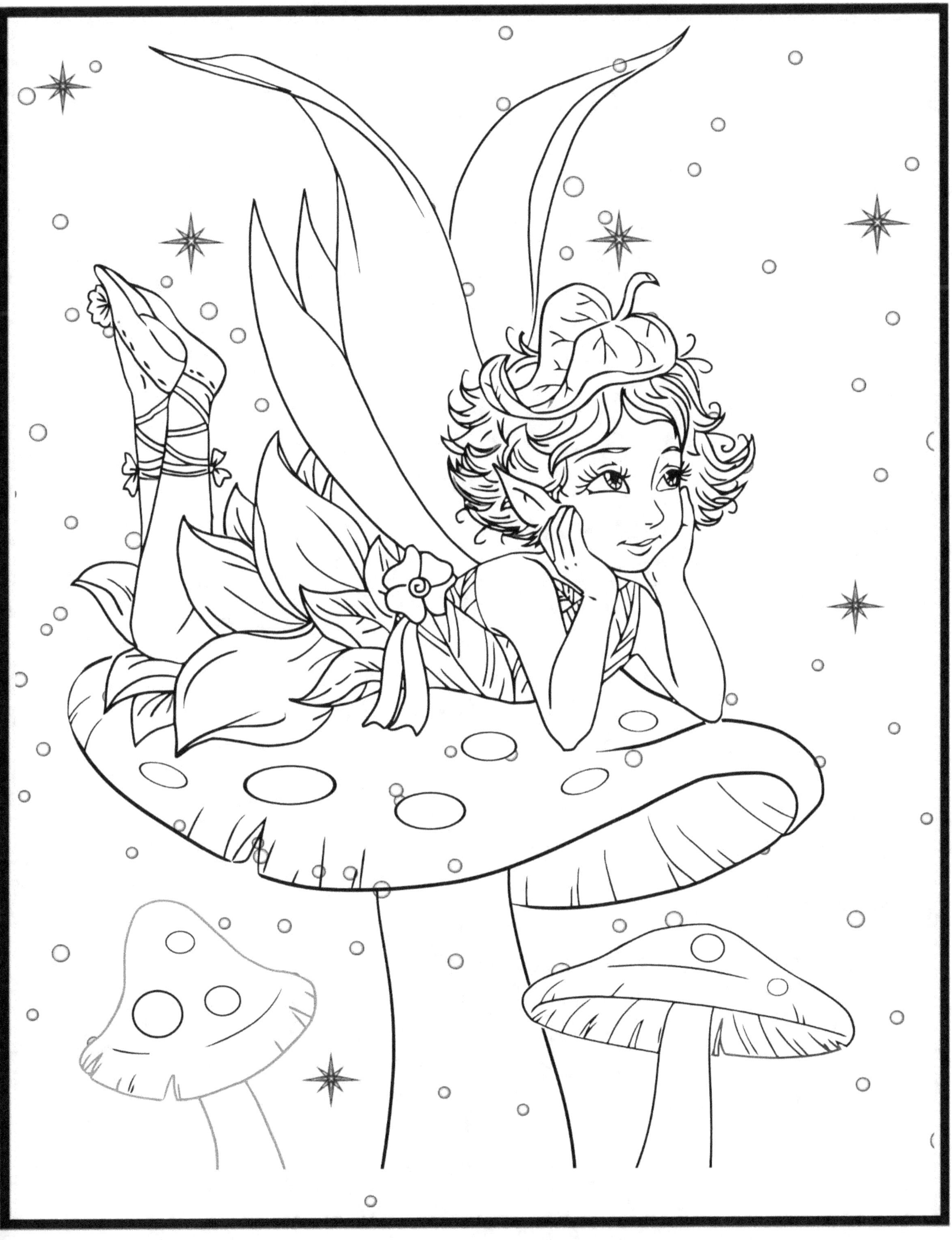

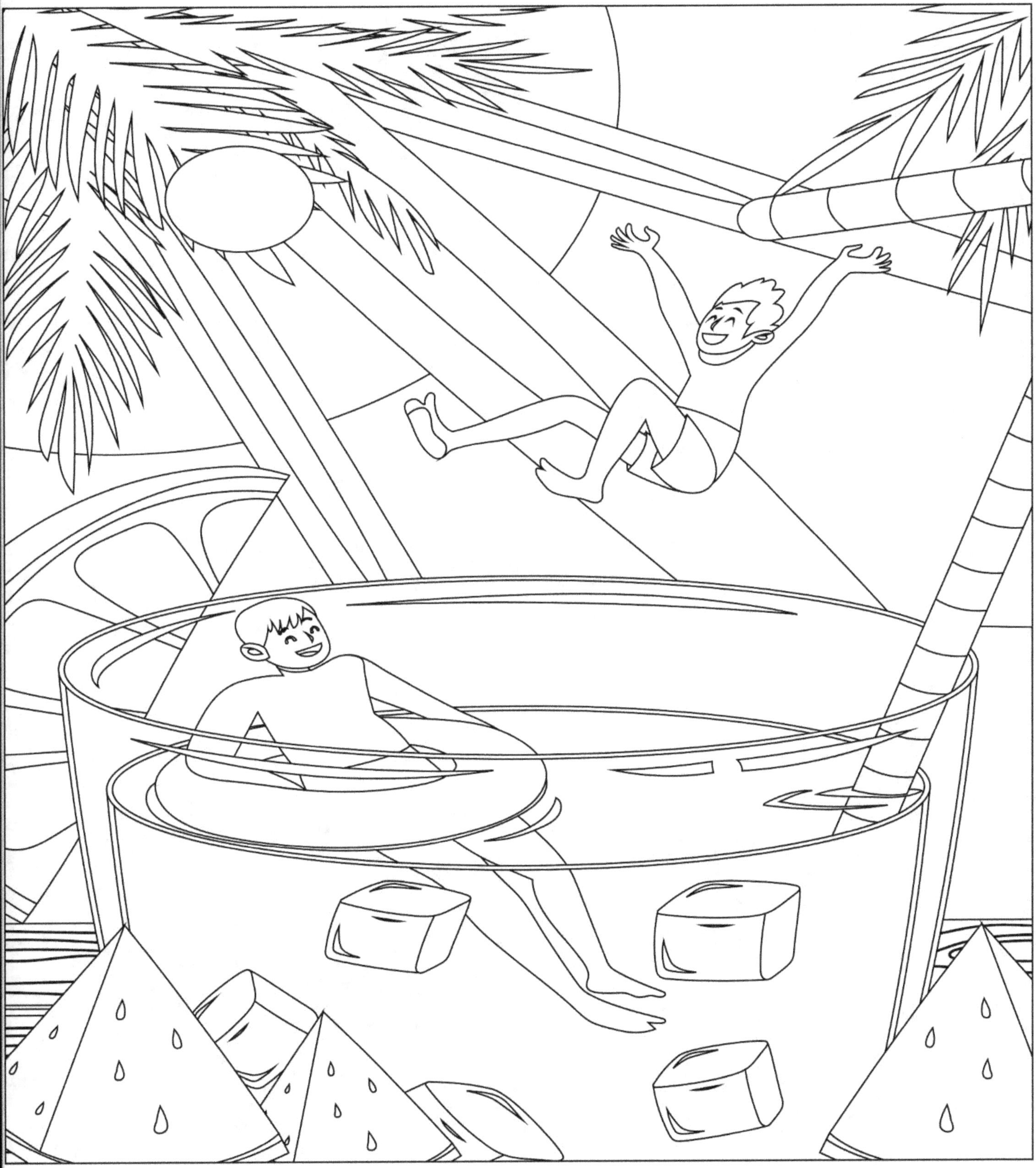

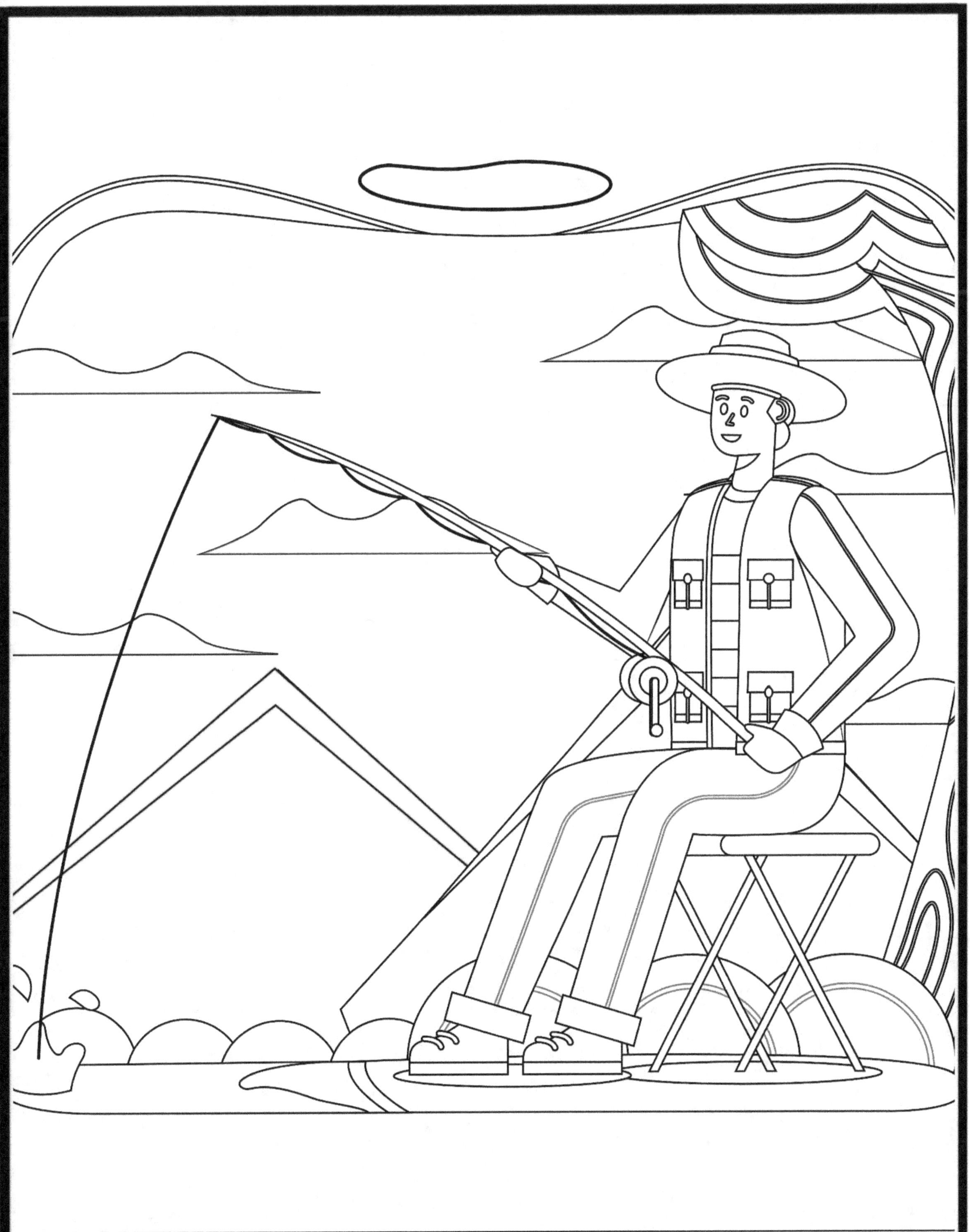

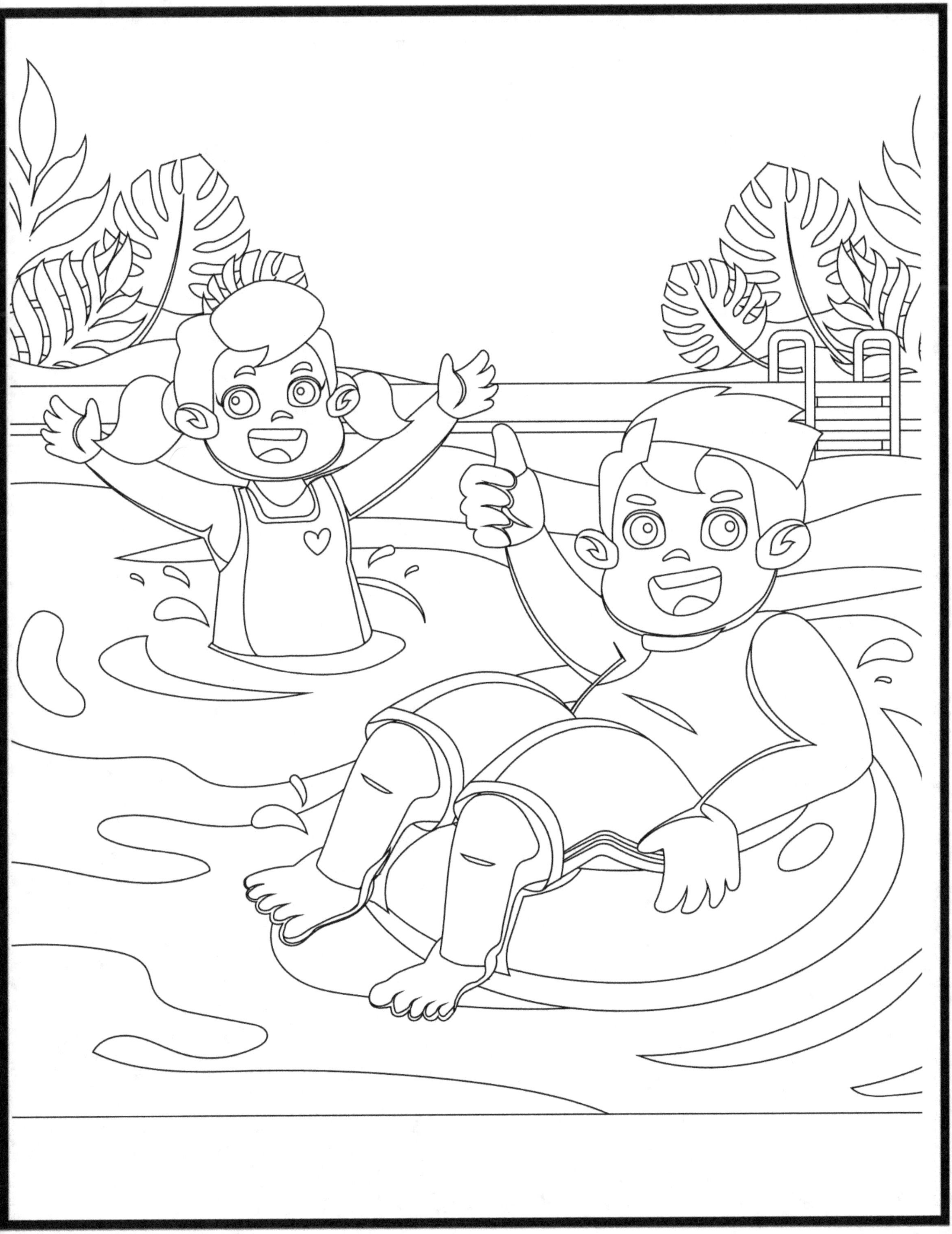

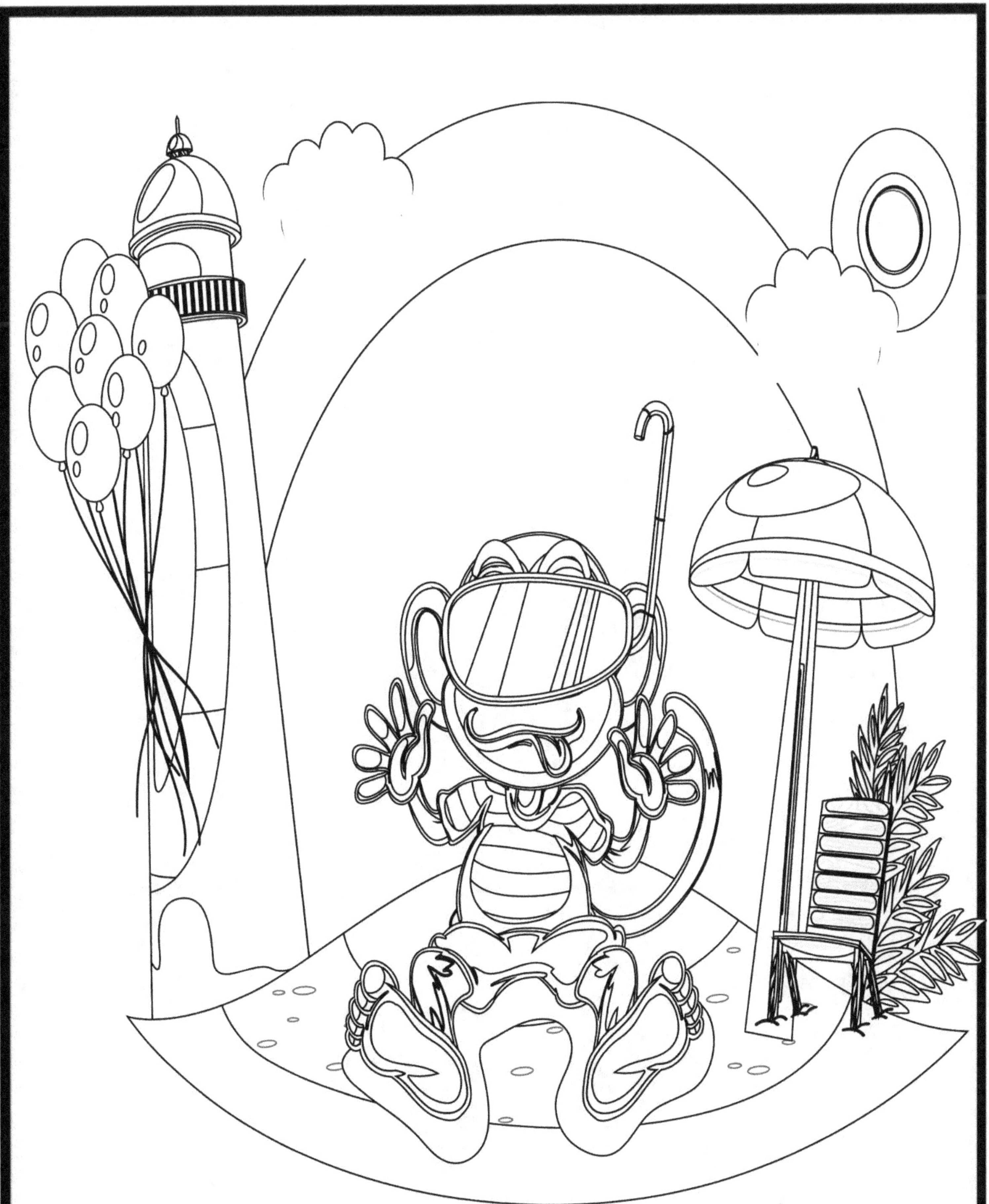

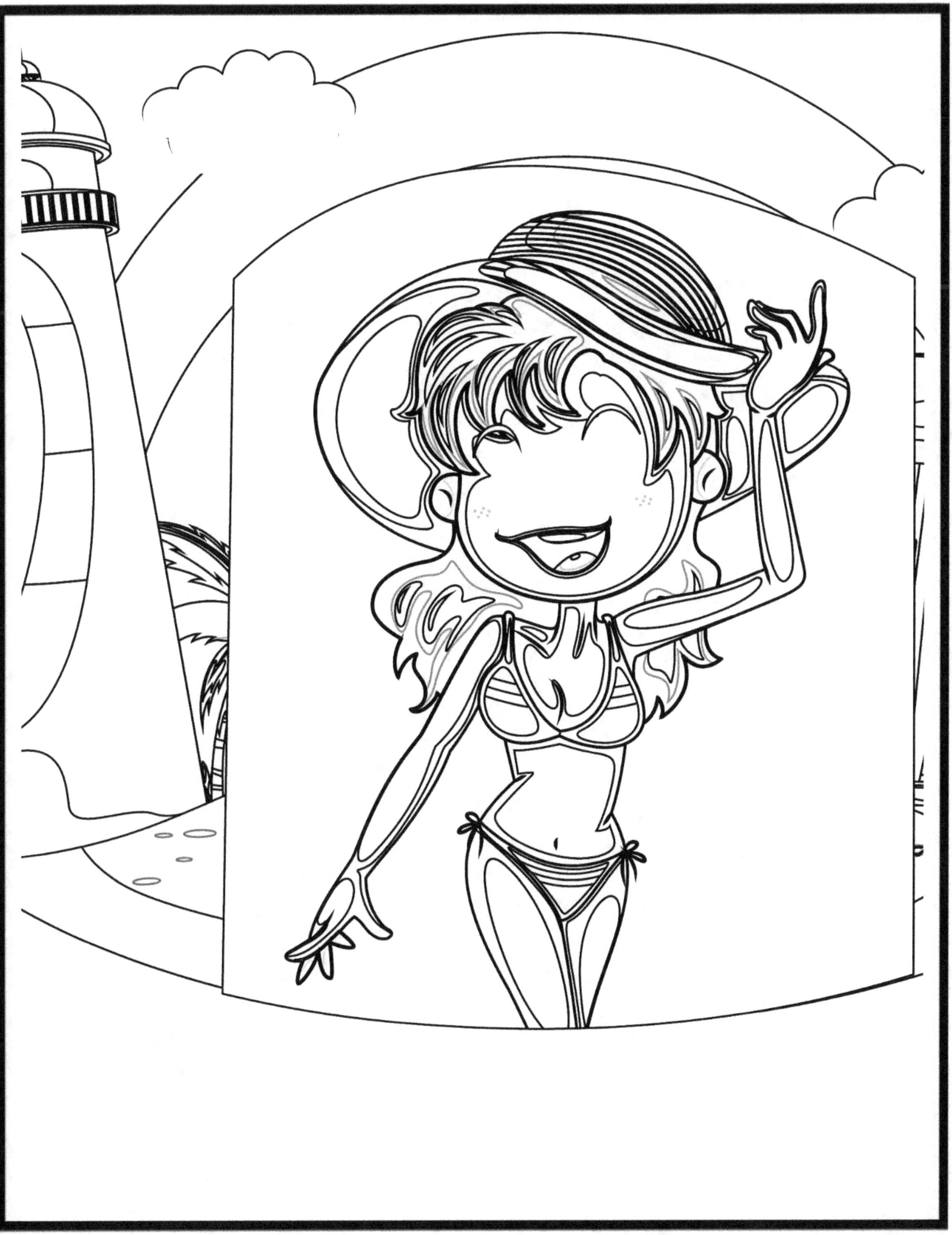

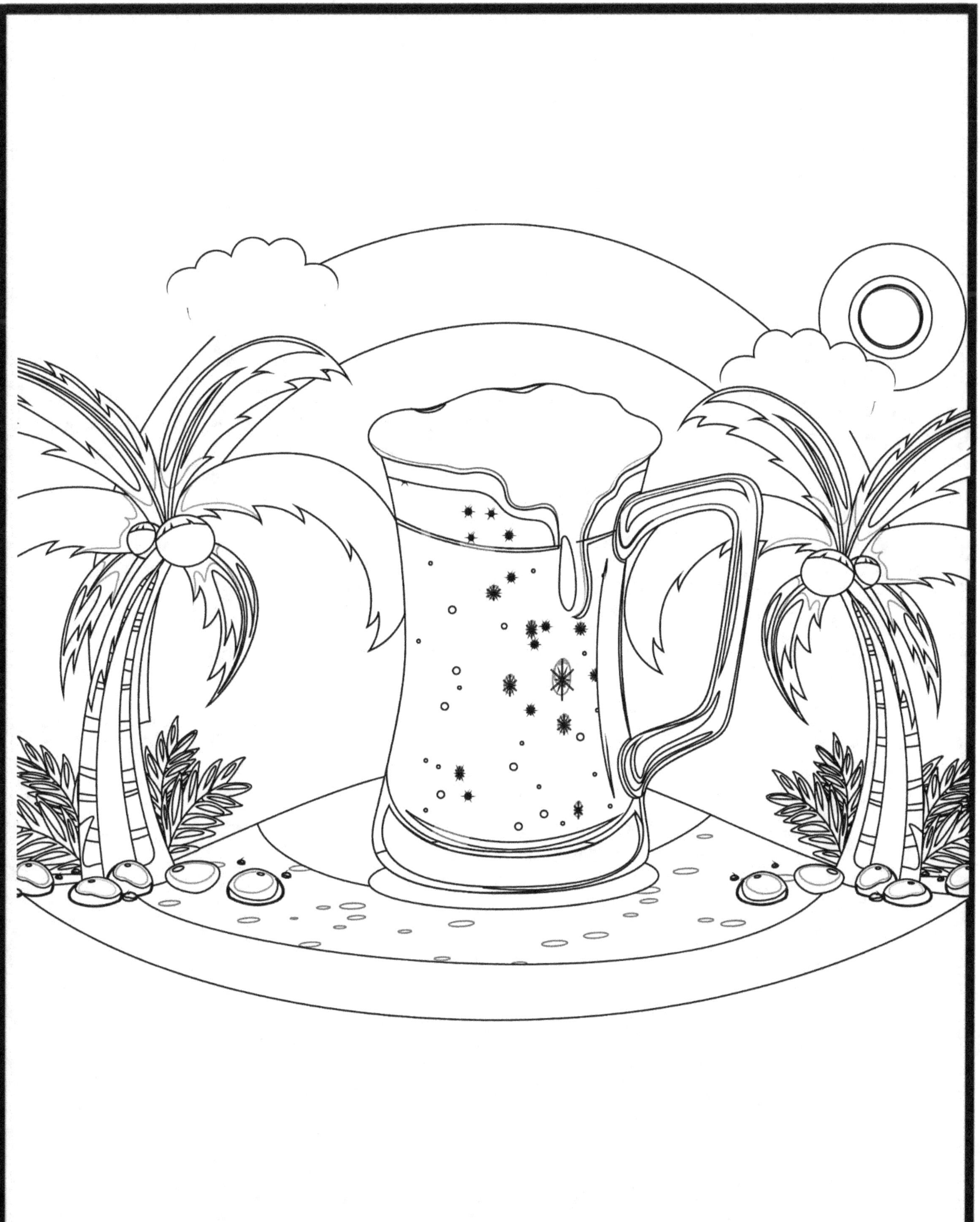

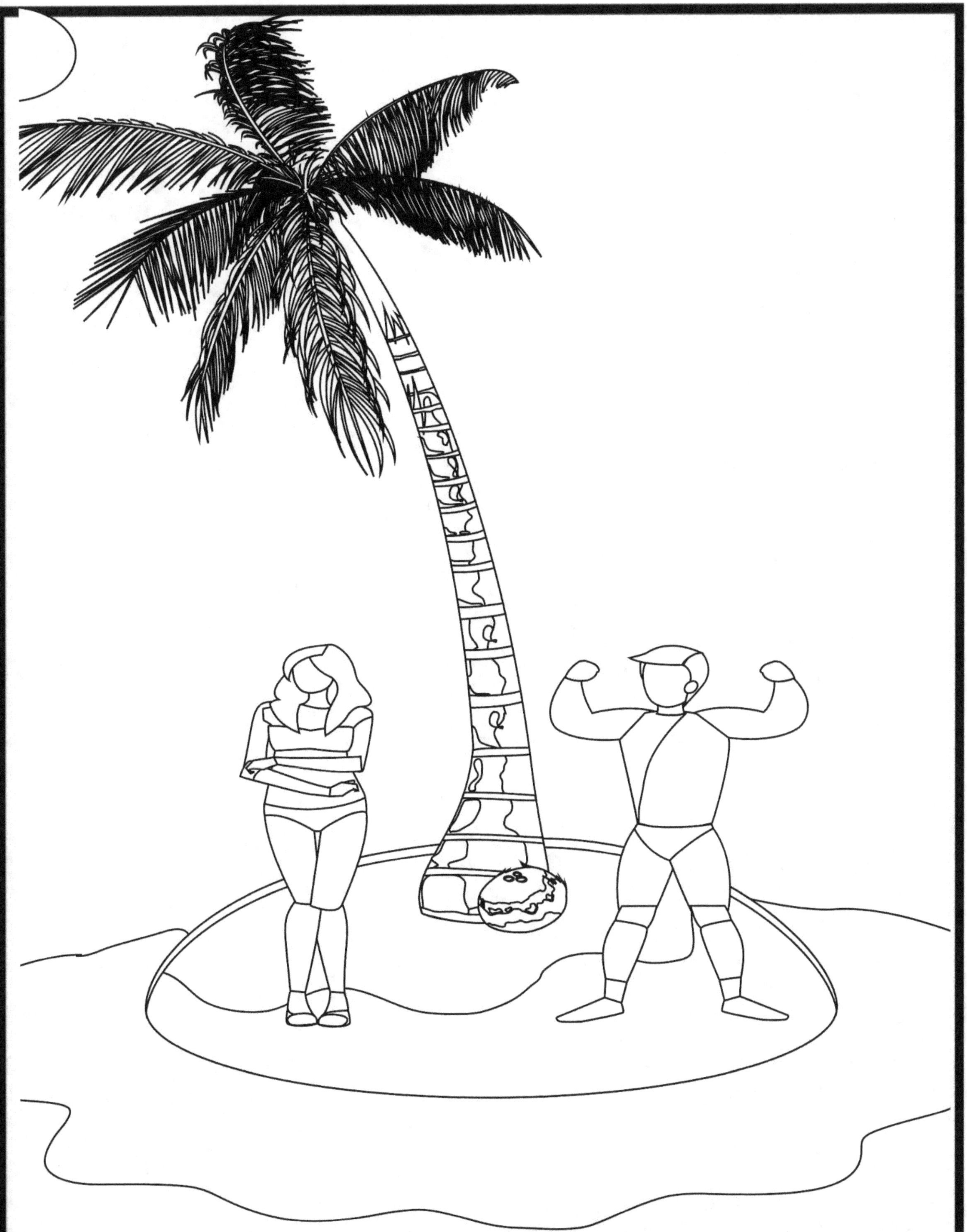

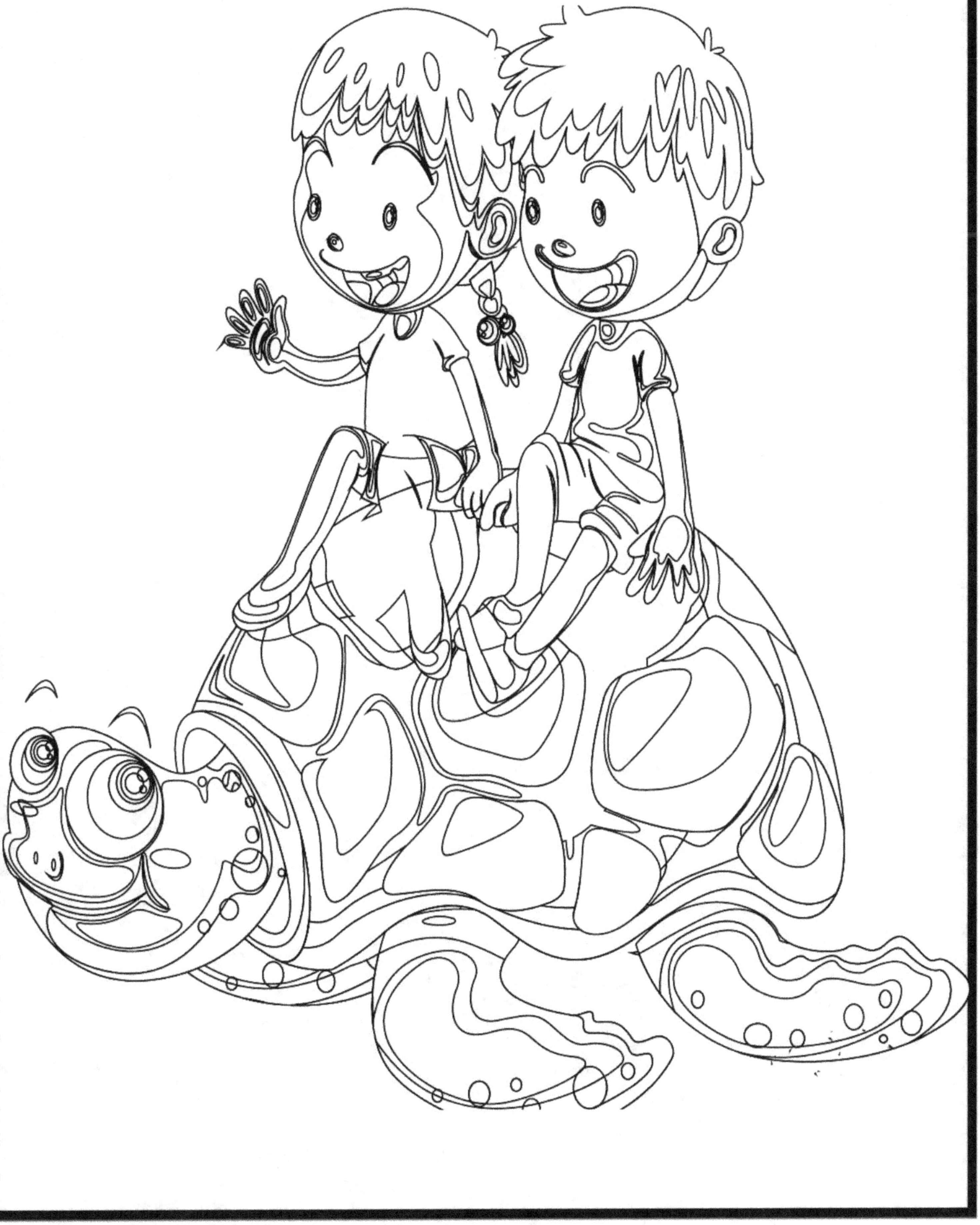

www.ingramcontent.com/pod-product-compliance
Lightning Source LLC
Chambersburg PA
CBHW081457220526
45466CB00008B/2678
9798509075513